ON THE COURT WITH . . .

DWIGHT HOWARD

DWIGHT HOWARD

By MATT CHRISTOPHER®
The #1 Sports Series for Kids

Text by Stephanie Peters

LITTLE, BROWN AND COMPANY
NEW YORK • BOSTON

Little, Brown and Company

Hachette Book Group
237 Park Avenue, New York, NY 10017
Visit our website at www.lb-kids.com

www.mattchristopher.com

Little, Brown and Company is a division of Hachette Book Group, Inc.
The Little, Brown name and logo are trademarks of Hachette Book Group, Inc.

First Edition: November 2010

Matt Christopher® is a registered trademark of
Matt Christopher Royalties, Inc.

Text written by Stephanie Peters

Cover photograph by AP/Wide World Photos

Library of Congress Cataloging-in-Publication Data

Christopher, Matt.
On the court with—Dwight Howard / Matt Christopher.
p. cm.— (On the court with—)
ISBN 978-0-316-08480-2
1. Howard, Dwight—Juvenile literature. 2. Basketball players—
United States—Biography—Juvenile literature. I. Title.
GV884.H68C47 2010
796.323092—dc22
[B]
2010008622

10 9 8 7 6 5 4 3 2 1

CWO

Printed in the United States of America

Contents

★ PROLOGUE ★

Sticker Slap

On February 17, 2007, four talented players in the National Basketball Association (NBA) competed in the Slam Dunk contest. The players were defending champion Nate Robinson of the New York Knicks, Tyrus Thomas of the Chicago Bulls, Gerald Green of the Boston Celtics, and Dwight Howard of the Orlando Magic.

Of the participants, Howard was by far the biggest, standing at nearly seven feet tall and weighing in at 265 pounds. His size was no guarantee that he'd fly head and shoulders over the competition, but he wasn't nervous. "I have some tricks up my sleeve," he told reporters, a mischievous gleam in his eye.

Thomas opened the contest with a between-the-legs bounce pass that he caught off the glass and slammed through the hoop. The panel of five judges awarded him 37 out of a possible 50 points for the dunk.

Green, up next, enlisted the help of fellow Celtics player Paul Pierce. Pierce laid the ball up against the backboard. Green leaped, caught the rebound, and then circled the ball before jamming it home. That dunk earned him 48 points.

Now it was Howard's turn. He dribbled twice from the sideline near the three-point arc and then launched himself into the air for a one-handed windmill throw-down. The crowd roared with approval; the judges gave him 43 points.

Robinson finished the first round with a leg-twisting leap so high in the air that it looked as if he had launched himself off a trampoline. The move propelled him into second place, with 45 points.

Thomas, as the last-place holder, went first in the next round. He made a strong attempt—so strong, in fact, that he tore the net! But he was only awarded 43 points, giving him a total of 80 out of 100 points. Because only the top two point holders would advance to the final round, Thomas's chances to continue didn't look good.

Dwight Howard was up next. He jogged in from center court, took a lob pass from teammate Jameer Nelson, and with a mighty leap thrust the ball through the rim with his right hand. At the same time, he slapped his left hand against the backboard.

With that slap, he left behind a small sticker with a photo of his smiling face, his initials, his jersey number, and the Magic's team logo. The sticker marked the exact spot his hand had hit—an unbelievable twelve and a half feet above the floor!

But showing how high he could leap was just one reason Dwight Howard had left the sticker on the backboard. A closer examination of the sticker showed a handwritten phrase: "All things through Christ." By displaying his photo with that phrase, he was telling the world that he is a devout Christian. The phrase expresses his belief that everything he has accomplished and hopes to achieve is done thanks to the strength he receives from God.

Dwight is just one of many outspoken Christian athletes. Fellow basketball players Allan Houston and David Robinson, quarterback Kurt Warner, pitcher Orel Hershiser, and tennis player Michael Chang have all publicly embraced their religion.

The sticker also reveals another part of Dwight Howard. The smile that he wears in the photograph is full of fun, mischief, and optimism. That, according to his friends, family, and teammates, is Howard's personality in a nutshell. He's known for his goofy sense of humor and has no qualms in showing it on and off the court.

"Basketball brings me a lot of joy," he once told reporters. "Just knowing that I'm alive, and I have a reason to be here, brings me joy. Basketball is one place where I know I can be myself."

★ CHAPTER ONE ★

1985–2000

"Stop Smiling!"

"The Miracle Child."

That's what Sheryl and Dwight David Howard called their newborn son, Dwight David Howard Junior. They had long hoped for another child to join their family. But after several miscarriages, it seemed that their hopes would not be realized.

Then Sheryl became pregnant again. On December 8, 1985, she gave birth to Dwight.

"My dad always told me that I was a blessing," Dwight once told a reporter, "that I was called upon to do something in life."

The family lived in Atlanta, Georgia. Dwight Senior worked as a Georgia state trooper and volunteered as the athletics director at a small private school, Southwest Atlanta Christian Academy (SACA), where Sheryl taught physical education.

5

SACA's mission, to mix faith with learning, reflected the kind of education the Howards wanted their children to receive, so Dwight Junior entered as a kindergartner. He took to the school, its Christian ideals, and his classmates right away. He made friends who would stay with him throughout his school years and beyond.

While education and spiritual guidance were the primary focus at the school, SACA offered a wide variety of athletics, too. "My childhood was always centered around playing a lot of different sports," Dwight once said in an interview. "It was about playing every sport and staying active."

Dwight Junior was just three years old when he first picked up a basketball. In doing so, he was following in a family tradition. Sheryl had been the captain of the first women's basketball team at Morris Brown College. Dwight Senior coached youth basketball teams. Dwight Junior's sister played throughout school, too, and in college she helped her team to three Division II conference championships.

It's not surprising that Dwight took to basketball like a duck to water. But what was unusual was how much effort he put into teaching himself how to play.

To improve his dribbling, for example, he sometimes set up chairs or orange cones on his street and wove through them with his eyes closed.

Dwight played other sports, but as he grew older, he realized that he preferred one above all others. "When I was about ten, I became really serious about basketball. I told my dad that I wanted to make it to the NBA."

Dwight Senior had been his son's basketball coach for more than four years. He had watched Dwight Junior develop as a player and teammate, and he believed that his boy just might have what it took to make it in the big league. He told Dwight that he'd help him achieve his goal in any way he could. Sheryl echoed those sentiments with just as much enthusiasm.

But was Dwight Junior really willing to put in the hard work necessary to make his dream come true?

Dwight Senior usually thought so. There were other times, however, when he would glance at his son during a practice or a game and just shake his head and sigh. It wasn't that Dwight Junior was misbehaving, or slacking off, or making the same foolish mistakes over and over. But he was doing something that made his father just as crazy.

"Stop smiling out there!" Dwight Senior would yell. "Why can't you take the game seriously?"

The thing was, Dwight Junior *did* take the game seriously—so seriously, in fact, that after a loss, he'd often break down and cry. Defeat bit him to the quick, but it also made him even more determined to win the next game.

Ten-year-old Dwight played basketball as often as he could. He joined every team possible, in school and with the local Amateur Athletic Union (AAU) league. He attended summer basketball camps. When organized games weren't available, he pitted himself against older basketball players in pickup games.

"They were a lot smarter and stronger," he remarked of his experience as a fourth grader playing with eighth graders, "so I learned. They pushed me around a lot to see where my head was and see if I would back down."

Driven by his willingness to learn, Dwight continued to improve. By middle school, his ball-handling skills, quick feet, and heads-up play made him a natural at point guard. Yet as good as he was on the court, Dwight recognized that his physical abilities were only part of what he'd need to reach his dream.

"The Bible says to have your vision and make your plan so the whole world can see it," Dwight said. So when he was in eighth grade, he wrote up his plan on a page of notebook paper. He worded his goals like a proclamation in the Bible. Among them were the following:

And it shall and will come to pass that SACA will win the 2002–2003, 2003–2004 state championship.

And it shall and will come to pass that Dwight Howard II will be the Number 1 draft pick in the NBA draft.

And it shall and will come to pass that Dwight Howard II will surpass LeBron James for the best high school basketball player, college player, and NBA player.

It shall and will come to pass that the NBA will be run by the standards of God.

Amen.

Dwight tacked the notepaper to his wall, where he would see it every day, a constant reminder of what he believed himself capable of achieving.

Not everyone believed in him the way he believed in himself. Sometimes even his closest friends doubted his ability.

Dwight squashed those doubts when he was in eighth grade. At five feet, ten inches, he was one of the tallest boys in the school. But his build remained that of a skinny adolescent. None of his friends thought that he had enough muscle to dunk.

Dwight told his friends to meet him at a local basketball court. When they were all assembled, he grabbed a ball and said, "Watch this!" To his friends' astonishment and delight, he leaped sky-high and dunked!

"It didn't move the rim or the backboard, and the net didn't even shake," Dwight recalled. "I was still happy about it, though."

So were his friends, many of whom were also his teammates. *If Howard can dunk the ball in eighth grade,* they must have been thinking, *imagine what he'll be like when he's playing on the high school team!*

That Dwight would make the SACA varsity basketball team seemed obvious. After all, he was already outplaying many of his older classmates. But not many believed that the scrawny twelve-year-old from an unknown Christian school was NBA material.

A few years later, however, people found themselves looking at Dwight Howard in a whole new way.

★ CHAPTER TWO ★

2000–2002

From Medium Guard to Extra-Large Forward

Sometime between the ages of twelve and sixteen, boys go through a growth spurt. Their shoulders broaden, their feet get bigger, their arms and legs lengthen, and they add weight and muscle to their frames. By the time they reach their late teens, they start looking less like boys and more like men.

A person's height—like hair color, eye color, and body shape—depends a lot on genetics. A boy whose family tree has many tall people is usually above average in height. Typically, a boy won't grow that much taller than the others in his family.

Of course, there are always exceptions.

Between eighth grade and freshman year of high school, Dwight had grown from five feet ten to just over six feet tall—and he wasn't done growing. During his freshman year, he stretched to a towering six feet, nine inches tall, a full five inches taller than his father!

Some boys would find it difficult to adjust, physically and mentally, to such a sudden and dramatic change in their bodies. Dwight seemed to take it in stride. He stayed active, which helped him remain in control of how his body moved. His friends and his family, his devotion to his religion, and his determination to give whatever he did his best effort helped him wade through the murkiest waters of adolescence.

Dwight hadn't hit the peak of his growth spurt at the start of his freshman season. So his coach, Courtney Brooks, made him a point guard for the Southwest Atlanta Christian Warriors.

That position suited Dwight just fine. He had long admired a famous NBA guard, Magic Johnson of the Los Angeles Lakers. "I used to watch Magic all the time," Dwight once said, referring to a series of instructional videos Johnson made called *Magic Fundamentals*. "I did what he did on the tapes, all his dribbling moves....I always wanted to be like Magic."

Thanks in large part to Dwight's skills, the SACA Warriors had a winning season that year. Unfortunately, his summer team wouldn't benefit from those same skills. In June, Dwight broke his leg and was forced to sit out summer ball, as well as two basketball camps he'd planned on attending.

Such a long layoff can leave a player rusty. Luckily, when Dwight returned to the court for his sophomore year, it was as if he'd never been sidelined. He now stood at six feet, nine inches tall. His height was such a great advantage that Coach Brooks moved Dwight to the forward position.

Dwight wasn't upset with the move. "I knew I wouldn't play point guard anymore," he said, "because I was bigger than everyone else."

Still, Dwight continued to hone his ball-handling and play-making skills while working even harder to strengthen his rebounding and blocking abilities. He practiced his shooting, too. He was naturally left-handed, but after breaking his left wrist in eighth grade, he taught himself to shoot righty. Now, he could easily alternate with his right and left hands. He also practiced dodging around defenders to make a shot. If real players weren't available,

Dwight just pictured an opponent standing between himself and the basket.

In short, Dwight was building himself into every coach's dream—a versatile player who could "read" the court and make things happen. He took inspiration from the game's best players, a list that included Michael Jordan, Shaquille O'Neal, Tim Duncan, and his personal favorite, Kevin Garnett.

Garnett's aggressive style of play attracted the sophomore. So did the path he had taken to the NBA. Garnett had chosen to skip college and jump right into the league out of high school.

Dwight began to wonder if he could follow that same path. His sophomore year stats of 16.5 points, 12.5 rebounds, and 6 blocks per game were certainly on par with other top high school players in the nation. But unlike those players, there was no guarantee that Dwight would ever be noticed by any basketball scout, college or professional. That's because most scouts simply hadn't heard of SACA and therefore, had no reason to visit it.

No reason, that is, until the following year. That's when Dwight Howard burst onto the scene and took their breath away.

⋆ CHAPTER THREE ⋆

2002–2003

Junior Sensation

Take a look at Dwight Howard today and you'll see a mass of solid muscle, from his broad shoulders to his powerful legs. Coupled with that strength are graceful athleticism and startling speed for a man his size.

If it were possible to go back in time, one would see a much different person.

"I was a really skinny kid," he recalled. "My dad [took] me to the gym and I couldn't bench-press one plate."

Dwight began hitting the weight room to add muscle to his frame. Doing so wasn't easy, however, because he had grown even taller, to six feet, ten inches! With so much of his body's energy going toward growing *up*, there just wasn't a whole lot extra for growing *out*.

16

Still, Dwight managed to bulk up. That strength, plus his height, helped him improve his per-game averages from the previous season, to 20 points, 17 rebounds, and 7 blocked shots.

Dwight was happy with those stats, but not with the way the Warriors' season ended. A glance at one of his goals explains why: *And it shall and will come to pass that SACA will win the 2002–2003 state championship.*

In the final days of his junior year season, his goal had been within reach. Southwest Atlanta Christian had powered their way into the Class A boys' state championships for the first time. They were beating Whitefield Academy throughout much of the match. But in the last four minutes of the game, they fell apart. Dwight himself got into foul trouble. Final score: Whitefield Academy 83, Southwest Atlanta Christian, 72.

Dwight was disappointed at being runner-up instead of champion. But he didn't have time to dwell on the loss for long, for after high school basketball ended, AAU basketball began.

The seventeen-year-old was a member of the Atlanta Celtics, an AAU youth basketball program that had a reputation for molding stellar players. Dwight played well during the spring schedule, but it was during the squad's summer tour that he emerged as one of those stellar players.

The summer schedule began with the Tournament of Champions in North Carolina. The TOC was a major basketball event for the AAU. The Atlanta Celtics were one of sixty-four teams in the seventeen and under age bracket. These teams were divided into sixteen pools of four. Each team played the others in its pool once. The squad that emerged at the top of its pool then played in the National Playoffs, a knockout round that left the two best overall teams standing.

Those two teams were the Pump 'N' Run squad from Southern California and the Atlanta Celtics from Georgia. They met for the championship match on Sunday, May 25. Dwight Howard, along with his teammates Josh Smith and Randolph Morris, sparked the play for the Celtics early on. But that spark fizzled out too soon. Smith and Morris had trouble making their shots. Dwight did his best to make up the difference, but it takes a whole team to win a basketball game. In the end, the Pump 'N' Run players outscored the Celtics 94–86.

Once again, Dwight had to be content with runner-up.

In June, Dwight traveled to Virginia for the NBA Players Association Top 100 High School Basketball Camp, a six-day gathering for select high school students. In an arena filled with talent, Dwight absolutely shone. He dazzled the camp's coaching staff, the visiting NBA players, and the college and pro scouts. Behind his power, his team, the Spurs, made it to the camp's championship game. But once more, he found himself in the role of runner-up when the Spurs lost to the Rockets.

Dwight's performances on the court had been so phenomenal that he was voted the camp's top player. Suddenly, scouts who had never heard of Southwest Atlanta Christian Academy were pulling out their maps so they could track down the phenom from Georgia.

Dwight Howard was officially on their radar. Now it was up to him to stay there.

★ CHAPTER FOUR ★

Summer 2003

"Total Domination"

Dwight Howard continued to spark interest in the last weeks of June that summer. But it was in the second week of July that his name became the one on every basketball recruiter's lips.

Dwight was in New Jersey for the prestigious adidas ABCD camp. Founded by Sonny Vaccaro, the man known for matching star players with sneaker companies, the camp sought to bring together talented high school players, respected college coaches, and NBA scouts.

In going to the ABCD camp, Dwight Howard was following in the footsteps of some very famous players. Kobe Bryant, LeBron James, and Kevin Garnett had all risen to superstardom at the camp. All three had also made the jump right from high school to the pros after their outstanding performances at the ABCD camp.

Knowing this, Dwight set himself a single goal for the days ahead: "Total domination."

He dominated, all right, impressing campers and recruiters alike from day one.

"He's a beast," one camper exclaimed. "It's like his hands are webs or something."

"He just looks like somebody who'd kick everyone's butt," a recruiter raved.

The week of camp ended with the traditional Senior All-Star Game between the Black and Gold squads. Dwight, playing for the Black, helped his team win the contest 165–153 by ripping down nine rebounds. His shooting for the evening wasn't great, but that didn't stop recruiters from top colleges from talking to him. Dwight was willing to listen and even stated that he'd like to win the NCAA championship someday.

But he made no promises to anyone because with each passing day, his lifelong dream of going straight into the NBA was closer to becoming a reality.

Immediately after the ABCD camp, Dwight was

reunited with the Atlanta Celtics for the adidas Big Time Tournament in Las Vegas, Nevada. The Big Time was exactly as its name implied—BIG. Four hundred teams, or an estimated 5,500 athletes, played a total of 996 games on thirty courts. The teams were placed in one of four divisions: Open, A, B, or C. Of these four, the Open Division was the top-ranked. The Atlanta Celtics were in this division.

The Celtics went undefeated throughout the opening days of play. But of course, as they advanced up the ladder toward the championship game, the competition grew tougher.

The Atlanta Celtics were pretty tough themselves, however. Dwight Howard, Josh Smith, and Randolph Morris played together like a well-oiled machine. Like Howard, Smith and Morris were both going into their senior year of high school; like Howard, they were very tall, standing at six feet nine and seven feet, respectively. Together, the threesome made a formidable front line that devastated the opposition.

Their first game in the final round was against the Connecticut Select. It was no contest: After thirty-two minutes of play, the Select were headed for the showers, having lost 93–68.

Next up were the Rotary Select I from the state of Washington. They fared a bit better against the Georgians, but still lost 87–73. The Atlanta Celtics had made it to the championship game!

Their opponents were the Michigan Mustangs. The Mustangs were a solid team, and at first, it looked like the match was going to be close all the way.

It wasn't. The Celtics pulled away in the seventh minute and never looked back. Sparked by phenomenal shooting and rebounding efforts from Howard and Smith, they drove their lead up to 15 points by halftime. The Mustangs simply couldn't stop them. Final score: Atlanta Celtics 85, Michigan Mustangs 65.

"This is a tremendously special group of guys," Celtics coach Karl McCray enthused after the victory. "We have never had a more talented group than this one."

Strong shooting certainly played a huge part in the Celtics' victories. But defense was just as important and there was no one better than Dwight

Howard. In the three-game championship round alone, he came down with a rebound an astonishing 31 times, or an average of just over 10 boards per game! Smith was strong in that stat category as well, with 18 boards in the final three games. In recognition of their performances, Howard and Smith were jointly awarded the Open Division Outstanding Player Award.

Howard, Smith, and Morris continued to play well in the final weeks of the summer competition. At the Best of the Summer Tournament in Los Angeles, California, they helped the Celtics romp past seven teams before, disappointingly, falling in the semifinals. Exhaustion may have played a part in that loss. Dwight recalled phoning home and saying, "I just want to get back to my own bed."

The loss hardly detracted from the impression the Atlanta Celtics made overall. "The best summer team I've ever seen," one college coach said.

And the best of the best that summer was, hands down, Dwight Howard. He'd set out to dominate, and he'd succeeded. But would that success carry him to his ultimate goal, namely, to be the number one draft pick of the NBA?

★ CHAPTER FIVE ★

2003–2004

The Buzz Builds

After the summer games of 2003, the basketball world was buzzing about Dwight Howard.

"Dwight is the most versatile big man I've seen," adidas ABCD camp director Sonny Vaccaro said. "[He] will be number one. I've never been so sure of something."

"He is the best player in the country, by far," recruiting analyst Bob Gibbons agreed.

Vaccaro and Gibbons were joined by other scouts and recruiters in praising Dwight. Their admiration wasn't only for his jaw-dropping basketball skills. They also appreciated the way he handled himself off the court.

"He's just a grounded kid," one scout said of Dwight. "You won't have to worry about him speeding in a foreign car or getting drunk."

"Simply just a real nice kid," Gibbons echoed.

It would have been easy for all the praise and attention to go to Dwight's head. He could have started acting like a big shot at SACA. Yet he remained much the same as he'd always been—just a nice, humble teen.

"I was taught to always respect other people, whether they are young or old," Dwight explained. "Just treat them with the same respect you want somebody to treat you."

One thing did change, however. His morning routine became a bit more complicated.

At the start of his senior year, Dwight began working out in the mornings with a personal trainer. It wasn't always easy for him to drag himself out of bed at four o'clock. But he did it, knowing that every time he went through a series of drills, every time he ran a lap around the track, he was moving one step closer to his NBA dream.

"Hard work negates errors," he reflected about these dawn sessions. "You have less chance of failure."

After the early morning workout, Dwight drove to Southwest Atlanta Christian in a nine-hundred-

26

dollar 1984 Ford Crown Victoria. He wore the school uniform and began his school day with prayer. He was an attentive student and had a grade point average of 3.2 (out of a possible 4.0). He sang in the school choir, earning him the nickname "Choirboy," and served as copresident of the student body.

"This school is just filled with love," he once said of SACA. "All of these people here are like family to me."

When Dwight wasn't at school or on the court, he behaved just like any other teenager. He played video games or went bowling or to the movies with his friends. His favorite flick? Disney's animated movie *Finding Nemo*.

"It's a great movie!" he told a reporter years later. "My favorite character is Dory. She's silly and makes me laugh. I love kids' movies because I'm a big kid."

Dwight's "big kid" personality made him a favorite with the students, the teachers, and the administration at Southwest Atlanta Christian.

"He's always courteous and always smiling," Geraldine Thompson, the school's headmistress, remembered.

His coach, Courtney Brooks, used words like "humble" and "nice" to describe his star player. "As a person, I would duplicate him ten times over," Brooks said.

Another administrator recalled the kindness Dwight once showed her son. The boy was a top student, but when the day came for him to receive an honors award, he was more embarrassed than proud of himself. "But when Dwight stood up and clapped for him," the administrator recalled of the ceremony, "that made [my son] feel good."

The way Southwest Atlanta Christian treated its athletes helped Dwight remain grounded. "Our school was not basketball first," Dwight's Warriors teammate Austin Dudley explained. "It was school first."

Still, as the 2003–2004 basketball season drew near, it became clear that Dwight was going to be blitzed by the press. Dwight Senior and Sheryl realized that while they couldn't stop the media flood, they could control it.

They assembled a team of advisors that included Dwight's uncle, Paul Howard, a district attorney in Atlanta; the Howards' pastor, who provided spiritual guidance; and their accountant, who gave financial advice.

Protected by this phalanx of family and friends, Dwight had the freedom to concentrate on his last year of high school. He also had time to consider the path he wanted his future to take—college or pros? But before he chose, there was something he had to do first.

Champion

One of the goals Dwight Howard Junior had set five years earlier was still ringing in his ears: *And it shall and will come to pass that SACA will win the 2002–2003, 2003–2004 state championship.* The Warriors had fallen short of that goal in 2003; Dwight was determined that would not be the case in 2004.

"Right now, I'm just worried about winning basketball games," he told anyone who asked about his future plans. "My team is what matters the most, not who is watching."

Dwight was the spark that fueled the Warriors that season, but the team had plenty of firepower besides him. Sophomore point guard Javaris Crittenton was a formidable player, with fellow guard Daryl Slack, forwards Aljamon Alexander and Austin Dudley adding to the team's might. With ample help from the bench and expert coaching by Court-ney Brooks, the squad soared through the first months of the season.

Dwight had several standout games, including one against the Berkmar Patriots that saw him going 14-for-15 from the floor on his way to a 36-point total. He also had 15 rebounds, 6 blocked shots, 5 assists, and 1 steal that night. He added a moment of levity, too, when he approached the Berkmar team and began to congratulate them on playing a good game. The Patriots — and the Warriors — just looked at him in confusion because it was only the end of the third quarter!

Southwest Atlanta Christian had an undefeated record by the beginning of December. Many games were blowouts; even teams that had troubled them in the past, such as Whitefield Academy and Land-mark Christian, now fell before them.

It wasn't that the other teams weren't good. They just couldn't compete at the same level with the Warriors. And as good as some of their players may have been, they didn't stand a chance against Dwight. He played with a confidence and athleti-cism beyond his years. He earned double-doubles in several games, and a few times hit double digits in three categories.

But he wasn't looking to rack up his own stats. He was looking to win games. If the shot wasn't there, he'd pass off to a teammate. "He'd tell them that if they missed it, he'd get the rebound and let them shoot it again," Coach Brooks recalled. "That's why he's the ultimate team player."

That winter, the Warriors played in two prestigious national tournaments. The first of these was the Slam Dunk to the Beach, a holiday basketball showcase that featured twenty-two of the best high school teams. To come out on top, the Warriors had to play their best every night.

They did just that—for the most part. They clipped the wings of the Thunderbirds from Provo, Utah, with a 68–55 victory. Dwight came close to a triple-double with 25 points, 21 rebounds, and 9 blocked shots. Two of his points came off a particularly daring move.

Thunderbird Matt Pinegar remembers the play well. He was hot on the heels of a Warriors guard he suspected was going in for a layup. He wanted to be in good position for the rebound if the shot missed.

But if the guard had intended to shoot, it was the worst shot Pinegar had ever seen. The ball didn't kiss the glass and bank in gently; it rocketed off the backboard.

"What is he doing?" Pinegar recalled thinking.

What the guard was doing was setting up Dwight Howard for a monstrous dunk. A split second after the ball ricocheted off the board, Dwight leaped over Pinegar, plucked the ball from the air, and stuffed it through the hoop.

Pinegar knew then that he was in the presence of a great player—and a good guy, too, for Dwight didn't gloat after his dunk. Instead, he smiled broadly as he hustled back on defense.

"He has fun out there," Pinegar commented about Howard.

Plays like that dunk made for exciting basketball at the tournament. So did tremendous comebacks. Southwest Atlanta Christian didn't usually find themselves on the wrong side of the score, but in their match against Arlington Country Day of

Florida, they dug themselves into an 18-point hole. Dwight and his teammates pulled together, prevented ACD's seven foot two center from scoring a single point, and won.

The Warriors won their other matches, too, until only one opponent stood in their way. Reserve Christian Academy from Reserve, Louisiana, was the surprise of the tournament. They had beaten much higher ranked teams, including the number one squad in the country, to reach the finals.

Their Cinderella story ended there, however. Dwight Howard saw to that. He scored 26 of his team's 71 points and had 21 boards. Those, numbers, combined with the stats of his quarterfinal and semifinal games, earned him averages of 24.7 points, 22.0 boards, and 6.3 blocks.

As Coach Brooks told a reporter during the tournament, "He just does everything."

After the Slam Dunk showcase tournament, the Warriors traveled to California for the Pangos Dream Classic. The one-day event showcased five games between pairs of teams loaded with talent. Dwight Howard was one of the biggest draws.

Southwest Atlanta Christian played in the fourth

match against Dominguez High of Compton, California. Dominguez did what no other team had done so far that season: They beat SACA, 66–52.

Losing wasn't something any of the Warriors cared to have happen again that season. But it did, and on national television.

Sports network ESPN2 broadcast the game between SACA and Landmark Christian Academy of Georgia. The star of Landmark's squad was Randolph Morris, Dwight's Atlanta Celtics teammate. It was a duel between the big men from the opening minute.

Boom! Slam! Whap! For every dunk, rebound, and block Dwight posted, Randolph answered with one of his own. By game's end, they had each drained 25 points. But in the other stats, Morris came out ahead. Dwight had 11 rebounds and 4 blocks, while his counterpart had 15 rebounds and 5 blocks. Dwight might have chalked up more had he not fouled out, and SACA might have won. Instead, they left with their second defeat of the season, losing 73–71.

Soon after that loss, the Warriors reached the state championships for the second time. Dwight had fallen short of his goal the year before. This time he was determined to lead the Warriors to victory.

Southwest Atlanta Christian came on like gangbusters in the opening round of the playoffs. They declawed the Tigers of Commerce High with a devastating 83–38. Dwight was absolutely unstoppable, hammering down an unbelievable 9 dunks for 18 of his 21 total points!

"He's six-ten, we're six-five," Commerce's coach said matter-of-factly. "They could do what they wanted."

Next up was Warren County. They fell to SACA 76–42. Then came Emanuel County Institute. They fared better than either Commerce or Warren County, but still lost 76–62. The Warriors were in the finals!

Facing them for the state championship was Whitefield Academy. In earlier meetings that season, SACA had beaten Whitefield 67–63 and 70–47. It was anybody's guess how this final match would go.

It didn't take long to find out. In the opening minutes of the March 6 showdown, SACA forced Whitefield to turn over the ball seven times on their way to a 17–5 lead. Dwight didn't score a single point in those eight minutes, but in the second quarter, he came alive. By the half, he had 12 points, plus 6 blocks and 9 rebounds. The Warriors headed to the locker room with a comfortable 35–22 lead. They continued to dominate in the second half as well, widening the gap to 15 points. In the end, Whitefield didn't stand a chance. Final score: Southwest Atlanta Christian 63, Whitefield 45.

Dwight's performance that night had been jaw-dropping: triple-double figures with 26 points, 23 rebounds, and 11 blocks. That he scored more than a third of his team's points was even more remarkable considering he made them in just three quarters.

The championship victory marked the conclusion of Dwight Howard's career as a Warrior. His final averages of 25 points, 18 rebounds, and 8 blocks per game were outstanding and spearheaded the Warriors to a final record of 31 wins and just 2 losses.

Dwight's career as a Warrior was over, but he wasn't done playing high school ball — nor was he done being recognized as one of the best high school players in the country.

The honors started rolling in shortly after the championships. He was named the Naismith Prep Player of the Year, as well as the Gatorade National Player of the Year and Georgia's Mr. Basketball 2004. He was invited to play in the EA Sports Roundball Classic, as well as the adidas / EA Sports Superstar Boys All-Star Game. Although his team, the East, lost the Roundball match, he himself posted a double-double with 16 points and 12 rebounds. He was on the winning side of the Superstar game, chalking up a triple-double with 19 points, 14 rebounds, and 10 assists for the KG Superstars. His performance in that game earned him the MVP honors. Perhaps it was the fact that KG stood for one of his favorite players, Kevin Garnett, that he played so well!

Soon after the Superstar game, Dwight took to the court for the McDonald's All-American Game. Joining him on the East team were his AAU teammates Josh Smith and Randolph Morris. The threesome conjured up their old magic to crush the rival West squad 126–96. The star of the show that game wasn't Dwight, but Josh, who drained 25 points. Dwight was strong, too, however, adding 19 points and 10 rebounds. The two were declared co-MVPs in recognition for their stellar play.

Dwight wasn't finished collecting awards, either. He was named McDonald's National High School Player of the Year and elected to the *PARADE* magazine All-America Team. By then, every college recruiter and NBA scout was waiting to learn which path Dwight was planning to take, the one that led to college or the one right to the NBA.

What they didn't know was that Dwight had secretly made his choice many months before. All that remained was for him to tell his secret to the world.

✭ CHAPTER SEVEN ✭
2004

The Announcement

On April 15, 2004, an audience of five hundred people packed into the gymnasium of Southwest Atlanta Christian Academy to hear Dwight Howard make the most important announcement of his life.

The gathering began with prayer. Then Dwight, his eyes full of tears, took to the podium and told the world that he was entering the NBA draft.

"I promise I'll be a ballplayer you'll be proud to watch, and a young man you'll be proud to know," he solemnly vowed.

Dwight revealed later that he had made his decision to skip college even before his senior year began. "I didn't tell my teammates," he added. "I didn't make a big deal about going to the NBA, because I didn't want my school or my team just getting attention because I was going to the NBA."

Most basketball watchers believed that Dwight would be one of the top three picks in the draft. Dwight and his family hoped that he would be number one. But no one would know which team had the chance to choose him until May 26, when the results of the NBA draft lottery were announced.

The draft lottery system is a combination of team rankings, carefully calculated odds, and pure chance. There are thirty teams in the NBA. The fourteen with the lowest records take part in the draft. The worst-ranked team is given the number one slot, and so on down through the ranks. While the first slot team isn't guaranteed the first pick, its chances of getting the first pick are greater than the others' because of how the lottery is set up.

This is where the calculations and chance come in. Fourteen Ping-Pong balls, numbered one through fourteen, are put into a lottery machine. Each team is assigned combinations of four numbers such as 1-2-3-4 or 7-10-13-14 (the order doesn't matter). The team with the worst record is given the greatest number of combinations, 250 chances out of a possible one thousand, with the fourteenth team in line receiving only five.

At the appointed time, four balls drop into the chute. The numbers on those balls are then matched to the team holding that four-digit combination. That lucky team is then awarded the first overall draft pick.

On May 26, 2004, the four numbered Ping-Pong balls matched a number combination held by the Orlando Magic. Fans of the Florida team were overjoyed. In 2003–2004, they had suffered through one of the franchise's most dismal showings, a record of just 21 wins out of 82 games. They needed power, and now they had the chance to get it.

Dwight Howard was on Orlando's radar as a top choice, but so was Emeka Okafor of the University of Connecticut. Okafor had recently jumped into the limelight as the NCAA's Most Outstanding Player of the Final Four for his remarkable performances during the March Madness collegiate play-offs. Howard was the more powerful athlete of the two, but Okafor was the more experienced player thanks to his years in college.

In the days leading up to the draft, the Magic kept mum about who they preferred. "Neither is in front of the other," general manager John Weisbrod said.

Howard had plenty to distract him from the upcoming draft, including his high school graduation. Around that same time, he also appeared on the cover of *ESPN: The Magazine*.

"It was sweet," he recalled. "I remember looking at it and saying, 'Man, I'm in high school and I'm on the cover.' Our school was so small that once one person saw the cover, the whole school saw it."

His issue of *ESPN: The Magazine* hit the stands on June 7. Three weeks later, Dwight, his family, and a busload of his classmates and their parents drove nineteen hours to New York City for the draft.

Dwight remained hopeful that he would fulfill his longtime goal of being the number one pick. "I bring everything to the table," he told reporters, even as he noted that he needed to work on his overall strength. Still, he added, "you don't have to worry about me quitting on you just because I'm out of high school."

The evening of June 24, Dwight sat at a table in Madison Square Garden with his family. His body language—eyes darting, mouth set in a straight line, fingers twitching—spoke volumes about how nervous and excited he was.

At seven o'clock, the lights dimmed. A spotlight shone on the stage, where a gray-haired man was walking toward a podium. The man was NBA commissioner David Stern.

Stern cleared his throat. "With the first pick in the NBA 2004 draft," he said, "the Orlando Magic select Dwight Howard out of Southwest Atlanta Christian Academy in Atlanta, Georgia."

The crowd went wild. Dwight broke into a mile-wide grin. He hugged his parents and shook hands with Okafor. Then he strode to the stage to shake Stern's hand. "This feels so good," he cried.

He knew he hadn't been the odds-on favorite to be first pick, but he didn't let that spoil the moment. Instead, he looked upon it as a challenge. "I want to go out there and prove all the doubters wrong," he said.

Weeks after the draft, a fan asked Howard what his first reaction had been when he found out he was the first pick. Dwight's answer said it all: "Thank God I finally made it!"

⋆ CHAPTER EIGHT ⋆
2004

Rookie Warm-Up

Dwight Howard was once asked what the best thing about being a young NBA star was. Was it fame? Fortune? All the perks that come with being a celebrity athlete?

None of the above entered into his answer. For Dwight, the best thing was "being able to touch the lives of kids and teenagers across the nation. Some are about the same age as me, so we can relate to each other. I can have a positive effect on them."

Dwight wasn't just handing out some line. He believed in leading by example—an example that stemmed from his strong religious convictions. He had once set down a goal to bring the word of God as he understood it to the NBA. He knew that he would encounter some resistance to his beliefs. In fact, he had already faced one such challenge.

When he was younger, Dwight had drawn a crude picture of a Christian cross adorning the silhouetted player on the NBA logo. The press made a big deal out of that image when they learned of it. They claimed Dwight planned to push his religion on the league.

Dwight quickly made it clear that while he hoped to spread the word of God in the NBA, "that doesn't mean standing on a podium before a game and trying to tell everybody to follow Christ."

How did the Orlando Magic feel about Dwight's religious convictions? No one openly expressed any concern—and why would they? Dwight was one of the most mature, grounded teenagers ever to come out of the draft. If his beliefs played a part in that—and there could be no doubt that they did—then dissuading him from living by those beliefs would be foolhardy.

Two weeks after becoming a Magic player, Dwight reported to Orlando's summer league, where, he stated later, his "main goal...was to get accustomed to playing against bigger bodies."

Dwight had been weight training for a while, but now he stepped up his program so he could meet those bigger bodies with confidence. "I expect to take hits," he said. "But when I get back up, I just may hit them back. Harder."

He did well in the first five-game series of the summer league, earning the highest averages in rebounding (10.4) and blocks (3.0). He soared during the Magic's next summer stop, Las Vegas, where he scored 25 points and pulled in 9 rebounds in the final match.

Two months after the summer league ended, Orlando's training camp began. The practices were much longer and much more rigorous than any Dwight had ever experienced—and he reveled in every minute of them. In fact, he often put in extra practice time after the regular sessions were through.

"It was fun because I was doing something I loved," he said.

The NBA preseason began immediately after training camp ended. The Magic had made significant changes to its roster in the off-season. That the new crop of players was still trying to mesh was apparent during their first preseason games. They lost three in a row before finally pulling out a decisive

114–93 win in their fourth match. That victory was followed by three more to give the Magic a record of 4 wins, 3 losses.

In three of the seven games, Dwight had posted double-double figures in points and rebounds. He also added some crowd-pleasing dunks, including six in his first appearance. But his shooting from the free-throw line was inconsistent, and he got into foul trouble during one game.

Still, it was a respectable start for the rookie out of high school. But Dwight knew that he had to bring the good stuff to the court when the regular season began if he was to prove himself a true asset to the team.

⭐ CHAPTER NINE ⭐

2004–2005

"Dwight Howard Has Arrived"

On November 3, 2004, more than fifteen thousand hometown fans got their first glimpse of the Magic's number one draft pick, Dwight Howard.

Orlando's season opener was against the Milwaukee Bucks. The tip-off came at seven o'clock sharp. Moments later, the Magic's Steve Francis got the ball. He attempted a three-pointer from twenty-six feet out. *Clang!* The shot missed, drawing groans from the fans.

But those groans instantly changed to cheers when Dwight Howard captured the rebound. He jumped to put the ball through the hoop but was fouled on the shot. He went to the line hoping to put Orlando on the board first.

Unfortunately, he missed both free throws. To add insult to injury, Milwaukee's Dan Gadzuric nabbed the rebound after the second miss, passed to point guard Maurice "Mo" Williams, and then raced the length of the court. Williams fed him the ball and—*wham!*—Gadzuric slam-dunked for two points.

The Magic answered quickly with a three-pointer. The score seesawed between the evenly matched teams throughout the first half, finally landing at 50–47 in Orlando's favor when the buzzer sounded.

After the break, the Magic took control. Grant Hill threaded in a sixteen-foot jumper. Less than a minute later, Dwight stuffed the ball for his first slam dunk of the regular season. Five minutes later, the Magic had chalked up 10 more points. Dwight punctuated the run with another dunk to make it Orlando 66, Milwaukee 53. The jubilant hometown fans leaped to their feet, applauding madly.

But those same fans soon turned quiet as they watched Milwaukee slowly chip away at Orlando's lead until they knotted the score at 85 apiece. Dwight had a chance to score when he was sent to the line for two free throws. But as earlier in the game, he missed both. In fact, he didn't make a single free throw the whole night!

Those missed shots could have been very costly. With just three seconds left in the game, the Magic were down by one. They needed a miracle if they were to win.

They got it on their final possession. Grant Hill inbounded the ball to Steve Francis at the top of the key. Francis beat Mo Williams to the hoop and, with a mere 0.2 seconds on the clock, tossed in a sweet layup. Orlando won 93–92!

Francis was the hero of the game, but every player had done his part. Even with his missed foul shots, Dwight had been outstanding. In just thirty-eight minutes of court time, he posted a double-double with 12 points and 10 rebounds, plus 4 blocks, 3 steals, and 2 assists! "Dwight Howard has arrived," proclaimed one recap of the game.

Howard continued to impress the media, the fans, and his teammates throughout the month of November. He crashed the boards for double-digit rebounds. In one game, he nabbed an amazing 15 boards during an 18-point comeback run to beat the Los Angeles Lakers.

That same game saw him being "posterized" for the first time. A player is posterized when he attempts to defend against a dunk—and winds up looking foolish for even trying. On this night, Laker superstar Kobe Bryant was the dunker. As he drove to the hoop, Dwight slid under the basket, his arms raised over his head. Kobe didn't even hesitate; he leaped on top of Dwight, threw the ball two-handed through the hoop, and then clung to the rim with his legs hooked onto Dwight's shoulders!

"He baptized me," Howard confessed with a chuckle, "brought me into the NBA and back to reality with one play.... It was like 'Boom!' That's all I heard."

Two weeks after that, Dwight posted his highest-scoring game, with 24 points, while helping Orlando beat the Atlanta Hawks. The last of those points came with less than two minutes left in the game. Grant Hill, at the top of the key, passed him the ball. Dwight leaped and jammed it through the hoop with a massive dunk.

"He is neither awed nor intimidated by anyone he plays," the Magic's coach, Johnny Davis, commented later. "You think about his age and the fact he was in high school five months ago.... [Now] he's in there with the big boys."

Howard started off December on a particularly high note when, in a 129–108 win over the Toronto Raptors, he threw down 4 dunks and hit 7 of 9 free throws for 15 points. He also chalked up 3 assists, 2 steals, and 2 blocks. But his best stat of all was in the rebounding column. That night, he pulled down 6 offensive and 14 defensive boards for a total of 20! At just a few days shy of his nineteenth birthday, he was the youngest player ever to nab 20 rebounds. And yet—

"I'm not satisfied," he told reporters. "It's too early in the season. I would love to get 20 rebounds in a close game, instead of a game that was out of reach for the other team."

He got his wish two months later when the Magic faced the Atlanta Hawks on February 10. Orlando came on strong in the first quarter and racked up 31 points while holding the Hawks to just 15.

Orlando continued to dominate through the second quarter. But midway through the third, something happened. The Magic didn't score a single point in three minutes and only added four more before the buzzer sounded. The Hawks, meanwhile, had narrowed the gap from 20 points to just 6!

A come-from-behind victory for the Hawks suddenly didn't seem out of reach. If the Magic were to save the game — and their pride — they had to step it up.

They did just that. Steve Francis hit nine points midway. Grant Hill, Hedo Turkoglu, Kelvin Cato, and Doug Christie added to the score. So did Dwight, with a hoop-jarring dunk with less than four minutes remaining. The Hawks did their best to rally back, but it was no use. Final score: Orlando 101, Atlanta 96.

Dwight's last quarter dunk brought his point total to 15 for the night. Fifteen points is nothing to sneeze at, but it was his 20 total rebounds that really stood out. He was the first rookie since Tim Duncan in 1997–1998 to post two 20-rebound games.

"He was a monster down there," Steve Francis said admiringly.

Amazingly, it wasn't the last time Dwight achieved that mark in his first season. Shortly after the All-Star break in February, during which he played against second-year players in the got milk? Rookie Challenge (the Sophomore team won 133–106), he posted his *third* 20-rebound game. Despite Dwight's monumental effort, the match against the Toronto Raptors ended in defeat for the Magic.

In fact, many of Orlando's games ended in defeat in the final weeks of the 2004–2005 season. Dwight himself played inconsistently. He had four games in which he scored less than five points; in three of those games he pulled in eight or fewer rebounds. Yet he also posted back-to-back games of double-digit scoring and rebounding, plus a third that saw him chalk up 29 points, the highest scoring of his career at the time.

Unfortunately, that 29-point game ended in yet another loss. Orlando's front office had had enough. They fired coach Johnny Davis and temporarily replaced him with Chris Jent. Jent did his best to rally the team, but it was just too late. The Magic lost their final match to finish the season with 36 wins and 46 losses.

The team had known that 2004–2005 was going to be a building year. Now in the months ahead, they needed to grow even more to become a strong, well-oiled machine.

One of the most important parts of that machine was going to be Dwight Howard. Although he had stumbled at times, he had nevertheless shown his raw talent every time he stepped onto the court.

He had staying power—he was the first prep-to-pro player in NBA history to start in all 82 games in his rookie season. He had the talent—his 32 double-double games and averages of 12 points and 10 rebounds per game proved that. And he had the determination and the discipline to improve in the areas where he was weak. All he really lacked, Magic management believed, was experience.

Dwight himself knew that he wasn't at the top of his game yet. That fact came home even more clearly when the votes for Rookie of the Year were tallied. He lost out to his draft-day rival, Emeka Okafor of the Charlotte Bobcats, and runner-up Chicago Bull Ben Gordon.

Howard was disappointed by his third-place showing, but his fellow Magic teammates had nothing but good things to say about their rookie.

"Give him another year," Pat Garrity said, "and watch out!"

★ CHAPTER TEN ★

2005–2006

Sophomore Sensation

Dwight Howard's rookie season was behind him, but that didn't mean he hung up his sneakers. A few weeks after the Magic's final game, Dwight flew to the Philippines for the fifth annual NBA Madness, an event aimed at celebrating basketball with the Filipino people. He found the international travel exhilarating but made sure not to let it overwhelm him. When not taking in the local sights, playing basketball, or meeting people in his host country, he spent time reading, praying, and lifting weights.

He visited Hong Kong and Taiwan for similar events, but by August, he was back home in Florida to prepare for the coming season. He had packed on an additional twenty pounds of muscle in the off-season. His increased power showed early in the regular season. In the Magic's third game, he hit 17 points and made 11 rebounds, his first double-double of the season. Unfortunately, that third game was also Orlando's third loss.

The team turned it around in the next match, when they squeaked out a 76–74 victory over the Houston Rockets. Dwight Howard earned his second consecutive double-double, with 12 points and 11 rebounds that night. He posted a third in the next game, another win for the Magic, with 16 points and 13 rebounds, and added a fourth in the game after that, with 21 points and 16 rebounds.

On November 15, Dwight Howard and the Magic played the Charlotte Bobcats and Emeka Okafor. Howard and Okafor had met on the court a few times in 2004–2005. But this was the first time they would face each other since Okafor had been named Rookie of the Year. Basketball followers anticipated a heated battle — and they were not disappointed.

The two rivals met for the opening tip-off. Howard won and cannoned the ball to Steve Francis. Moments later, he swished a soft eight-foot jumper for the first two points of the game.

The Bobcats now had possession. They put the

High school phenom Dwight Howard shoots over a defender in the Jordan Capital Classic in April 2004.

The number one NBA draft pick of 2004: Dwight Howard holds up his new Orlando Magic jersey with the team's general manager, John Weisbrod (left), and his new coach, Johnny Davis (right).

Welcome, Rookie! The Orlando Magic's youngest player rises to great heights his first year in the league.

Make 'em work for every point! Howard tries to block a shot in a 2006 game against the Portland Trail Blazers.

Alone with the hoop, Howard throws down a dominating dunk!

Basketball buddies Jameer Nelson and Dwight Howard celebrate after Dwight stuffs a buzzer-beater to win a close game, 106–104.

Dwight "Superman" Howard shows his stuff in perhaps his most famous dunk, during the annual Slam Dunk contest in 2008.

The 2008–2009 NBA Defensive Player of the Year.

ball in Okafor's hands. He went up and missed! Dwight muscled in, nabbed the defensive rebound, and directed the play to the other end of the court.

Soon after that, Okafor fouled him. Dwight had spent a lot of time on his free-throw shooting during the off-season. That practice paid off now; he sank both shots. He added six more points in the following minutes, including a sweet hook shot from six feet out. He also pulled down six rebounds and helped out with an assist.

Emeka Okafor, on the other hand, had taken just one shot while committing two fouls. Of course, games aren't decided on the efforts of just two players. If they were, the Magic would have ended the quarter far on top. Instead, they were down by one, 20–19.

They were behind for much of the second quarter, too, until finally drawing even. When the buzzer sounded at halftime, the score was knotted at 46 points apiece.

Orlando unraveled the knot after the break. Charlotte drew even again and again in the next twelve minutes but failed to recapture the lead. The last quarter sealed the Bobcats' fate thanks to the outstanding play by Jameer Nelson. The sophomore guard came off the bench and made 11 of the Magic's 22 points!

Dwight added 4 of those points, too, plus 5 boards. The Bobcats simply couldn't withstand the Nelson-Howard one-two punch. Final score: Magic 85, Bobcats 77.

Dwight ended with an astonishing 21 points and 20 rebounds. He was only nineteen years old, making him the youngest player in NBA history to post a 20-20 game. That night was also his fifth consecutive double-double and his fourth career game of 20 boards. Any doubt that he had been the right choice as the first draft pick was laid to rest.

"Dwight played strong," Okafor, who had 8 points and 6 rebounds, admitted after the game.

Howard's teammates were a little more enthusiastic about his night's performance. "He's our Rookie of the Year," said Tony Battie.

How did Dwight himself feel about his efforts? "I just wanted to get the win," he told reporters.

In the weeks leading up to his twentieth birthday, Dwight got his wish for wins four more times. In each, he was the game's high rebounder, three times with double-digit figures. But sometimes, even his best efforts failed to result in a win. On November 29, he pulled down 19 rebounds—and yet, the Magic lost to the Chicago Bulls 85–76.

From there, the Magic spiraled downward. By the end of 2005, their record had dropped to 12 and 15. The team appeared on the verge of a rebound in January, when it had a streak of five wins. But hope of a playoff berth dimmed again soon after, for they lost ten games in the weeks before the All-Star break.

Fed up, Orlando management made a flurry of trades. Midseason changes to the roster are typically done when a team realizes it has only a small chance of reaching the postseason. The hope, however, is that after a short adjustment period, the team will begin to win games again.

That's exactly what happened with the Magic. They dropped eight of nine games right after the All-Star break, but then won ten of their next fourteen matches!

And the wins just kept coming. On April 15, Orlando won their eighth consecutive game, the thirty-sixth of their season.

That match, against the Philadelphia 76ers, saw Dwight Howard playing at his absolute best. How good was he that night? Here's a small sample:

The 76ers were up by one with three minutes remaining in the game. Dwight was fouled. He made the first of two free throws, missed the second, grabbed his own rebound, and sank a hook shot from eight feet out. That was three points in three seconds for the lead!

He wasn't done yet, either. Moments later, he ripped down a defensive rebound that Jameer Nelson converted for two more points. "It was the biggest play of the game," Sixer Allen Iverson said later.

By night's end, Dwight had chalked up 28 points, the most of any player that game, and 26 boards, the most of his career so far. To come close to 30 points or 30 rebounds in one game is amazing; to come so close in *both* categories is flat out unbelievable. *That's* how good he was that night.

If the Magic could just win their final two games, they stood a chance of reaching the playoffs.

Unfortunately, they didn't. Dwight played well in their next-to-last match, posting a game-high 14 rebounds and 22 points, but the Chicago Bulls ended their chances of a playoff berth once and for all by defeating them 116–112 in overtime. The final match, a loss to the Indiana Pacers, scarcely even mattered.

Dwight was very disappointed not to have made it into the playoffs. But rather than dwell on what might have been done, he focused on what needed to be done. More specifically, he focused on what *he* believed he needed to be doing to boost his own game—although a glance at his final stats shows that he was already doing plenty.

He averaged 15.8 points and 12.5 rebounds per game. His 1,022 total rebounds were the most of any NBA player that season, and they earned him a spot in the history books as the youngest person to reach that milestone. He also averaged 1.5 assists, 1.4 blocks, and 0.8 steals.

"That kid is a freak of nature," Kevin Garnett said of Dwight. "I was nowhere near that physically talented."

And yet, he wasn't satisfied with his performance that season.

"Shooting, rebounding, strength, conditioning," he told fans in an April online chat. "I need to work on my overall game.... I'd like to get better with my jump shot, and I'd also like to not turn the ball over so much when I'm double-teamed.... The Magic showed faith in me by drafting me number one right out of high school.... I'd like to pay them back."

And so, true to form, Dwight Howard set himself a goal: to develop his entire game in order to give the Magic their best shot at the title.

CHAPTER ELEVEN

Forging Ahead

As much as he smiles, Dwight Howard likes to make other people smile. He entertains his teammates with impressions of other players—he's especially proud of his Shaquille O'Neal—of his coaches, and of his favorite cartoon character, Dory from *Finding Nemo*. He plays practical jokes and practices his dance moves before the weight room mirror. He pokes fun at his friends. Once, he joked that his teammate, six-foot Jameer Nelson, wasn't tall enough to go on a new roller-coaster ride in Disney World.

"[He] didn't meet the requirements, so he had to stay home," he said with a wide grin.

Nelson had the last laugh, though—a video that showed Dwight hollering and screaming in terror throughout the ride.

On March 5, 2006, Dwight himself was given a

reason to smile. That's when he learned he had been named one of the twenty-three players of Team USA. If the team played well enough in international competitions in the next two years, they would go to the 2008 Olympics in Beijing, China.

"I always wanted to play in the Olympics," Dwight said.

Team USA traveled to Japan in August for the FIBA (Fédération Internationale de Basketball) World Championships. He and his teammates, who included NBA stars Dwayne Wade, LeBron James, Chris Paul, and Carmelo Anthony, won the bronze medal. Dwight started in five of the nine matches and contributed averages of 7.3 points, 4.7 rebounds, and a team-high 1.3 blocks.

After the FIBA World Championships, Dwight returned to Florida for training camp. Not surprisingly, he was showing signs of fatigue. The Orlando coaches limited his minutes during the practice sessions and the preseason games to give him time to recover from his travels.

That rest must have done him good because when he hit the court for the Magic's season opener against the Chicago Bulls, he was simply outstanding. He and his teammates pounded the Bulls in the first quarter, racking up 32 points to Chicago's 20. Four of those points were thanks to Dwight Howard's thunderous dunks. He also added points with a hook shot, a short jumper, and two free throws to reach double digits in just six minutes of play.

His hand stayed hot throughout the remaining thirty-six minutes, too. In all, he went 9-for-12 from the floor and hit 9 out of 10 free throws for a total of 27 points. Those free throws pleased him because he'd spent time perfecting the shot. His fans and teammates were happy with his other stats, too: 11 total rebounds, 3 assists, 2 blocks, and 1 steal. Even his opponents had to admire such an output.

"[He's going to] make it tough for anyone who comes into this building to get a win," Bulls center Ben Wallace said after the game.

Dwight really hit his stride mid-November. So did the Magic. Out of sixteen games played, they lost just four. Half of the victories were won by margins of ten or more points. Dwight was posting double-doubles night after night, including three games of more than 20 points and 20 rebounds.

The first of his 20-20 performances was particularly sweet because it came versus Kevin Garnett and the Minnesota Timberwolves.

"When I play against KG, it's like, 'Okay, this is the guy I watched growing up, wanted to be like,'" Howard said after helping defeat the T'wolves 109–98. "So I'm always excited to be on the court when I get to play KG."

Dwight himself gave people plenty to be excited about in the next weeks, including the game played on the night after his twenty-first birthday.

The match was against the Philadelphia 76ers. With just a minute and twenty seconds remaining, the score stood at 82–81 in Orlando's favor. A free throw by Grant Hill made it 83–81.

Hill missed his second free throw but darted forward, got his own rebound, and dished to Keyon Dooling. Dooling went up—but missed the shot!

Luckily, Howard snared the rebound and banked in a short shot. Two points, his twenty-seventh and twenty-eighth of the night! The Magic were up by four!

The Sixers shaved that small lead to the merest

whisker, but it was too little, too late. Final score: Orlando 86, Philadelphia 84.

Unfortunately for Magic fans, such victories were not the norm for December. From a 12–4 record in November, their win-loss column dropped to 18–14. In January it fell to 24–22, including eight losses out of their last ten games.

The Magic desperately needed a morale-boosting game. They got it from Dwight Howard in a game against the San Antonio Spurs and the Spurs' All-Star center, Tim Duncan. The Spurs dominated for most of the game, sometimes by as many as 16 points. In the third quarter, however, Orlando put the pedal to the metal and roared up alongside San Antonio to tie it all at 80 apiece.

Yet try as they might, the Magic couldn't take the lead. Then, with just five seconds remaining in the final quarter, Jameer Nelson stuck a thirteen-foot jumper to tie it up again. Moments after that, Dwight leaped sky-high and blocked the game-winning shot by Tony Parker! The ball cannoned into Nelson's hands—and Orlando immediately called a twenty-second time-out.

There were only 0.8 seconds left on the clock. "That's plenty of time for a pass, a good look, and a shot," one commentator noted.

Hedo Turkoglu prepared to inbound the ball near the top of the key. Dwight waited near the baseline with Duncan right on top of him. When the ref blew his whistle, Dwight circled around Duncan and back to the far side of the hoop. Duncan tried to follow, but he was a step too late.

Turkoglu lofted a pass at the basket. Howard jumped, arms outstretched, and *boom!*

"Alley-oop! Howard at the buzzer!" the commentator cried as Dwight bounced with happiness. "Dwight Howard climbs through the roof to put the Magic up!"

It was the first game-winning basket of his career, and left him with 30 points for the night. "Dwight had to go up and touch the clouds over Timmy," marveled one San Antonio player. "It was a remarkable play."

The NBA All-Star break came soon after that game. Dwight had played in the Rookie Challenge his first year in the NBA and for the Sophomore team in his second season. This year, he played for the East team and took part in the Slam Dunk contest where he performed his now-famous sticker slap. He gained fame of a different sort when, during practice, he launched into an impromptu dance-off with Shaquille O'Neal and LeBron James that had fans roaring with laughter. In the game itself, Dwight came off the bench to tally 20 points and 12 boards. It was an impressive double-double but did little to change the game's 153–132 West over East outcome.

After the break, the Magic slumped. They dropped thirteen of twenty games to send their record to 34 wins and 39 losses by the end of March. Dwight slumped, too, particularly on offense. In mid-March, he made 13 of 16 shots; the next night, he made just 2 out of 10. Just like the year before, their chance of reaching the playoffs was slipping away.

Then something happened. The Magic started winning again, and Dwight Howard was a big reason why. On April 7, he hit 31 points and pulled down 11 rebounds in a crushing 116–89 win over Memphis. Amazingly, 18 of his points came from dunks.

"This should help him get his confidence back," Grant Hill commented after that performance.

Howard certainly seemed confident a week later when he made all but one of his seventeen attempted shots in the first half of a game against Philadelphia. He finished the evening with a career-high 35 points, plus 11 rebounds, 5 assists, and 3 steals in the 104–87 blowout victory. It was his fifth consecutive double-double and his fifty-seventh of the season.

"I'm just happy I got a chance to really open up tonight and get going," Howard said with a grin.

His happiness that night was nothing compared to the joy he felt on April 18, the last game of Orlando's regular season. The Magic beat their homestate rivals, the Miami Heat, 94–68 to end with 40 wins and 42 losses. It was their best record since Dwight had joined the team and good enough to land them the eighth slot in the Eastern Conference playoffs.

That same night, Dwight entered the NBA history books as the second player after Wilt Chamberlain to post more than a thousand rebounds and a 60 percent or better shooting average in the same season. The Magic would need him to continue chalking up such strong stats in the postseason if they were to stand a chance against their first opponents, the Detroit Pistons.

✶ CHAPTER TWELVE ✶

April 2007

Under Pressure

"Dwight Howard has to have a big series and put up big numbers offensively."

"This contest looks like a complete overmatch with the Pistons being in the driver's seat."

"Detroit's championship poise will prove to be too much for Dwight Howard and the Magic."

Those were some of the predictions being made in the days leading up to the first round of the 2007 NBA Eastern Conference Playoffs. Such predictions were understandable.

The Detroit Pistons had a regular season record of 53 wins and 29 losses. The Orlando Magic had just 40 wins and 42 losses. The Pistons had beaten the Magic in each of their four meetings that year, with the most recent win coming just ten days before their first playoff match. The Pistons had several strong veterans, including high scorers Chauncey Billups, Rasheed Wallace, and Richard Hamilton. The Magic had their heavy hitters, too, but Detroit had a plan for handling them.

"We knew they didn't shoot very well from the line," Billups revealed. "So putting them on the line is a strategy."

That strategy called for them to target Howard in particular, whose free-throw percentage hovered just above the 0.500 mark. Hacking him made sense because it could throw off his game and remove him as a threat.

The Pistons were right—up to a point. Out of eleven free throws in the first match, Howard made just three. But those shots were just a small portion of his overall game, and in other categories, he played quite well. In fact, one of his plays made the Pistons very nervous.

The Magic had succeeded in closing a gap of 14 points to just 5 by the last minute of the game. Then Chauncey Billups made a costly offensive foul that put the ball in Orlando's hands.

That's all the Magic needed. Darko Milicic drilled a pass to Dwight, who was waiting under the basket.

Dwight leaped and—*wham!*—stuffed the ball through the hoop to bring Orlando to within three points.

That jam woke up the Pistons. They clamped down on defense, allowing the Magic just two more points. With just twenty-five seconds remaining, Orlando had no choice but to foul Detroit to send them to the line. If the Pistons missed, the Magic could get the rebound and convert for two.

But the Pistons didn't miss. Instead, Billups added five more points.

Final score: Detroit 100, Orlando 92.

The Magic lost two nights later by the same eight-point margin. Howard played only thirty-five minutes that game, and had just 8 points and 11 rebounds, causing many to wonder whether he was succumbing to the pressure of the playoffs.

Not so, his coach said. "Dwight was sick, quite honestly.... Before the game, he was nauseous and had intense stomach pains."

Howard was clearly over his stomach ailment when the Magic hosted the Pistons for Game 3. In the first quarter alone, he jammed three dunks to help Orlando match Detroit point-for-point.

But then he and the Magic lost steam. They were behind by 6 at the half and by 10 at the end of the third quarter, and fell apart in the last twelve minutes. The Pistons scored at will to add 22 points to their side of the board. The Magic tallied only 16. Final score: Detroit 93, Orlando 77.

Detroit now had a commanding 3–0 lead in the series. Orlando had to win all four of the remaining games to advance to the next round. They needed every single player to give his best performance every game.

They got just such a performance from Dwight Howard in Game 4. He picked apart the Pistons' defense and made 10 out of 15 shots. He was fouled frequently and while several of his free throws missed, 9 of them found their mark to give him a series best of 29 points.

He absolutely dominated under the hoop, too, ripping down a game-high 17 rebounds — 10 more than the Pistons' top rebounder. A pair of assists and an equal number of steals kept Orlando's momentum at a high. Midway through the third quarter, that momentum earned the Magic their first lead of the series. They fell below again five minutes later, but that lead had given them hope.

Dwight Howard gave them hope, too. His three-point play in the final minutes of the game boosted them back on top. But he also made mistakes that resulted in points for the Pistons. In the end, Orlando couldn't recover. The Pistons took the game 97–93.

There would be no second round in the playoffs for the Orlando Magic. As Dwight followed the progress of the other teams from the sidelines, he set himself a goal for the next season.

"Winning a championship," he told reporters. "That's my goal. I want to bring a championship to Orlando."

☆ CHAPTER THIRTEEN ☆
2007–2008

A Big Step Forward

Dwight Howard spent the summer of 2007 in the weight room, on the basketball court, and with friends and family. In late August, he played in the FIBA Americas Championship in Las Vegas, an Olympic qualifying series that ended with Team USA going undefeated in all ten matches. Dwight did his part, averaging 10 points and 5.3 rebounds per game.

The Magic, meanwhile, were just as busy. In early June, they hired a new coach, Stan Van Gundy. Van Gundy made some roster changes and brought in former NBA great Patrick Ewing as his assistant coach.

First and foremost on Ewing's list of responsibilities was to help Dwight Howard with his shooting. Howard was an expert dunker—in 2006–2007, he'd made more dunks than any other player in the league—but he wasn't very skilled in other shots.

"What kind of player do you want to be?" Ewing asked Howard soon after they started working together.

"The greatest," was Dwight's reply.

"Then you have to put in the work," Ewing told him.

And that's just what Howard did. He practiced running jumpers, hook shots, fadeaways, and layups. He shot them over and over with the goal of making the movement instinctive. That way, when the shot presented itself during a game, he would be ready to make it.

"I really like Patrick a lot. He's done so much with me already in the time that we've been together," he said of his mentor. "I can't wait to spend a whole season with him. I wish he could be here (in Orlando) until I'm finished playing."

The effect of Ewing's tutelage shone through in the Magic's first preseason game. In just twenty-nine minutes of play, Howard hit 13 of 20 shots from the floor, 4 of which were jump shots. The rest of his game was just as impressive: 11 rebounds, 4 blocked shots, 1 steal, and 1 assist. He also made 4 out of 6 free throws. Unfortunately, his hard work went to waste; Orlando lost the game 94–93 to the Atlanta Hawks.

That was their only loss of the seven-game pre-season, however. The regular season opener was another victory for the Magic, thanks to strong shooting from their newest player, Rashard Lewis, who put in 26 of Orlando's 102 points. Lewis credited Howard with helping him reach that number, saying the other team was so worried about keeping an eye on Dwight that they often left other players open.

Dwight, too, had a fine opening match, with 16 points, 12 rebounds, and 7 blocks in thirty-one minutes on the court. "To not even play in the fourth quarter and end up with 12 rebounds and 7 blocks is unbelievable," coach Van Gundy said.

At the end of November, Dwight reached a new personal best of 39 points in one game. Eighteen of those points came from massive dunks, raising his season total to 73. That was more than twice as many dunks as any other player—and more than many teams had made as a whole! Two nights later, he made 30 points and he ripped down 23 rebounds for a league-high fifteenth double-double and his second career 30-20 game.

Yet Howard would have traded it all in if only the game had ended in a win. Instead, the Magic lost to the Phoenix Suns 110–106 to finish with a record of 14 and 4.

After such a strong start, the Magic faltered in December. They had a pair of wins for a franchise-best record of 16–4, but then dropped three before defeating the Charlotte Bobcats. Dwight was a big reason they won that game. He had 33 points, 18 rebounds, and 4 blocks.

Yet not all was right with his performance. He was still struggling at the foul line. Eight of ten free throws were misses that night, leaving him frustrated.

"I don't know what was going on tonight," he said after the game. "I was shooting them hard, shooting them soft... [trying] to make my free throws as best as I could."

Nearly every other part of his game was going wonderfully, however. On December 28, at twenty-two years and twenty days old, he hit 29 points and pulled down 21 rebounds. It was the tenth 20-20 game of his career. Only Shaquille O'Neal had reached that milestone at a younger age.

The Magic chalked up their twenty-second victory on New Year's Eve with an edge-of-the-seat overtime win over the Chicago Bulls. The game might not have gone into extra minutes if not for the heads-up play of the Magic's star center-forward.

The score was 96–94 in Chicago's favor with thirty-eight seconds showing on the clock. The Bulls' shooting guard Ben Gordon had control when suddenly, *zip!* Out of nowhere, Dwight had stolen the ball! He fired it quickly to Jameer Nelson, who went up for a shot. *Slap!* Gordon fouled Nelson, sending him to the line for two free throws. Nelson hit both, and the score was tied!

Dwight was nearly the hero again in the last second of regulation time. With the score still knotted, he went up for a layup—but missed! Luckily, he nabbed his own rebound just as the clock ran out. Then Nelson and Hedo Turkoglu pushed the Magic ahead in overtime for the win.

Dwight had 17 points, 22 boards, 5 blocked shots, and 3 steals, including that key rebound of the game's end, that night. His coach called his effort "tremendous," a word that could also have been used to describe Howard's overall performance so far. He had improved in most categories since the same time the previous year. In December of 2006, he had averages of 16.8 points, 11.4 rebounds, and 1.9 blocks; now he had 21.7 points, 16.1 rebounds, and 2.9 blocks.

Two or more baskets per game from one player can mean the difference between a win and a loss. Dwight's extra points were definitely contributing to the Magic's winning season.

"If you make just a pretty good pass [to Dwight], he's going to do something alien with it, something out of this world," marveled his teammate Carlos Arroyo.

Spurred by Dwight's play, the team ended 2007 with 22 wins, up from 18 the previous season. By the All-Star break in February 2008, they had increased their victories to 33, while dropping just 21 games total. It was their best record in years and had many sports followers predicting good things for them come playoff time.

But that was several weeks away, and in mid-February Dwight had his mind on just one thing: the Slam Dunk contest.

✶ CHAPTER FOURTEEN ✶

February 16, 2008

Dunk King

In 2007, Dwight Howard tried but failed to win the Slam Dunk contest with his twelve-and-a-half-foot sticker slap. "The judges just didn't get it," he said. "I don't think people realize how hard it is for a guy to get 265 pounds up in the air and do some stuff."

This year, he was determined to wow everyone with his "stuff." His rivals for the prize were defending champ Gerald Green (now of the Minnesota Timberwolves), Jamario Moon of the Toronto Raptors, and Rudy Gay of the Memphis Grizzlies.

Moon and Gay took their turns first and ended up with scores of 46 and 37. Then Dwight approached for his shot. But he didn't move onto the court. Instead, he took the ball behind the backboard and lofted it up against the back of glass. As the ball rebounded back toward the stands, he leaped, caught it in his right hand, transferred it in midair to his left, and then, with his head still behind the board, jammed it through the hoop!

"Oooh!" the judges all yelled as one. Kobe Bryant, watching from the sidelines, reacted as if he'd been socked in the gut, grimacing in shocked admiration at what he'd just seen. Dwight received a perfect score of 50.

But Gerald Green's dunk had them cheering just as loud. As he dunked the ball, he blew out a candle on top of a cupcake that his teammate Rashad McCants had set on the back of the hoop. The judges were impressed, but not enough to give Green more than 46 points.

Gay and Moon took their second dunks a few minutes later. Gay ended up with a two-dunk total of 85, Moon with 90. Green went third and received 45 points for his move.

Dwight, meanwhile, was preparing for his second attempt. He marked a spot just inside the free-throw line with tape. As he did, Jameer Nelson approached carrying a bright red cape. Dwight pulled his team jersey over his head. Beneath his jersey was another blue shirt emblazoned with the Superman symbol.

The crowd went wild. The judges leaped to their feet, laughing and pumping their fists. Dwight Howard laughed, too, obviously delighted at the response.

"Superman is in the building!" one commenter bellowed gleefully as Nelson fastened the cape around Dwight's neck.

How super was Dwight? He launched himself so high in the air from so far away that he truly seemed to soar to the basket! It was another perfect dunk worth 50 points.

Moon and Gay were now out of the contest. Green went first in the final round. He accepted a high-lobbing pass from behind the backboard and swooped it through the net with power and grace. It was an impressive move, and yet, it didn't earn him top marks.

Not so when Dwight took his shot. He arced the ball from midcourt to a spot on the floor below the hoop. As the ball flew through the air, he dashed forward, jumped, and caught it in his left hand at the top of its bounce. Still in the air, he tossed the ball gently against the glass, caught it in his right hand, and stuffed it. The move demanded perfect timing, a soft touch, and pinpoint accuracy, and Dwight delivered on all three counts.

"I'm leaving the building!" the commentator roared. "I'm quitting my job! I've never seen anything like that!"

Green followed up with a sock-footed slam, but by then everyone knew the night belonged to Dwight Howard. His final jam, in which he plucked the basketball from a mini-hoop mounted next to the big hoop, was just the icing on the cake.

"I don't think people want to see the same old dunks," Howard said after accepting the trophy. "They want to see something else, see some spice."

Dwight Howard had added "spice" to the contest; he brought it to the table in the weeks that remained in the regular season, too. So did the rest of the Magic. They tore through the competition to a final record of 52 wins and only 30 losses, good enough for third place in the Eastern Conference.

Dwight had been masterful. By season's end, he had earned a shooting average of 20.7, a full 3 points more than the previous year. His block average was the best of his career so far, 2.1 per game. He played in all 82 games for the fourth year in a row, bringing his total games-played figure to 328.

"I've never seen a big man with his stamina," coach Van Gundy once said of Dwight.

But it was Howard's amazing rebounding talent that put him head and shoulders above the rest. On April 15, he pulled down his four thousandth career rebound, making him the youngest player to achieve the milestone. He was also the youngest player to lead the league in rebounds, with a total of 1,161 and an average of 14.2 per game. That was an increase of more than 150 boards from 2006–2007, and 124 more than the second-place rebounder that season.

"I really didn't think about the rebounding title," Howard confessed later, adding that he was more excited about reaching the four thousand mark. "That was something I couldn't imagine in such a short time in the league."

Of course, there was only one title he really wanted that season, that of NBA Champion. But did he and the Magic have enough depth to stand up to the ferocity of that competition? They would soon find out.

✸ CHAPTER FIFTEEN ✸
2008

Playoff Magic

The 2008 NBA Playoff series between the third-seeded Orlando Magic and the sixth-seeded Toronto Raptors opened on April 20 in Florida. The two teams had met three times in the regular season, with the Magic coming out on top twice. Toronto's sole win had been decisive; however, it was anyone's guess which team would emerge victorious in this postseason matchup.

Dwight Howard and Raptor Chris Bosh faced each other for the opening tip-off. Dwight won and sent the ball directly into Jameer Nelson's waiting hands. Nineteen seconds later, Nelson drained a three-pointer from twenty-five feet out to get Orlando on the board first. Hedo Turkoglu followed with four points. Then Maurice Evans, a shooting forward Orlando had acquired from the Lakers in a midseason trade, stuck a three-pointer. Rashard Lewis duplicated that effort with a three-point jumper of his own. Moments after that, Dwight lofted a seventeen-foot jump shot that hit for two points.

Less than four minutes had ticked off the clock and already the Magic had 15 points! It was truly a team effort, with all five starters contributing to the score.

The Raptors, meanwhile, had only eight points. They added just 15 more in the remaining minutes for a first quarter total of 23. Orlando, on the other hand, tallied an unbelievable 43 in the first twelve minutes of play! Dwight had a hand in all eight of the last points, assisting on 2 three-pointers by Keyon Dooling and adding a bucket of his own right at the buzzer.

Toronto did their best to battle back, but by half-time, they were still in a hole by 13. That margin might have been even greater had Nelson and Howard not bobbled several plays in the final minutes. Luckily for Magic fans, they were back in good form after the break. So were the rest of the Orlando players.

But the Raptors had woken up by then as well. They cut the Magic's lead to eight with a minute and a half left in the third quarter. They edged even closer in the fourth quarter, drawing to within five points two minutes in. With the momentum shifting in Toronto's favor, Orlando called a time-out.

Whatever Stan Van Gundy said on the sidelines clearly made an impact on his players. *Swish!* Turkoglu hit from twelve feet out. *Boom!* Howard thrust down a dunk. Forty seconds later, he ripped down an offensive rebound and kissed the ball to the glass for a layup. And then he banked in another two-pointer to make it six straight points in ninety seconds! He followed up those plays with a steal that he dished to Jameer Nelson—who stuck the ball through the hoop for two more points!

The Raptors tried everything they could to stop the Magic, but nothing worked. Final score: Orlando 114, Toronto 100. Series score: Orlando 1, Toronto 0.

The entire Magic squad had put on a show of strength, but Dwight Howard was the best of them all. His totals of 25 points, 22 rebounds, and 5 blocks for the night earned him a place among the elite:

Only eleven other players in NBA history had posted such numbers in a playoff game.

"It felt real good," a tired but elated Howard said. "Actually, I almost got some tears."

Two nights later, it was the Magic who nearly "got some tears" when the Raptors roared back from an 18-point deficit to tie it before halftime.

But the Magic were not to be denied. For six minutes in the third quarter, Jameer Nelson and Dwight Howard put on a scoring show. Jameer scored a three-pointer; Dwight tipped in a basket for two. Howard added a free throw; Nelson stuck two from the line. Howard made back-to-back buckets; Nelson made back-to-back three-pointers — and suddenly, the Magic were on top by nine points!

The Raptors clawed their way back again, however, to take a one-point lead with just 1:04 showing on the game clock.

It was edge-of-the-seat excitement in the final minute of the match. Turkoglu made a layup and then two free throws to put Orlando up by three. Then, with nine seconds left, Raptor Carlos Delfino rolled in a layup to cut the lead to a single point!

Orlando had to be very careful not to foul Toronto

or commit a turnover. If the ball got into the Raptors' hands, a single basket would mean the game.

Toronto had a chance for that single basket after an offensive foul. Fortunately — for Magic fans, anyway — Raptor Chris Bosh missed his nineteen-foot jumper. Orlando won 104–103 to go up two in the series.

Dwight, meanwhile, left the court with his second 20-20 playoff game, with 29 points and 20 rebounds. Only four other players in thirty years had achieved that milestone; the last player to do so was Howard's idol, Kevin Garnett. "Since the last game," he said later, "the only thing on my mind, when I go to sleep, when I wake up, at the gym with the guys, is to dominate."

But dominating was not in the cards for Howard or the Magic in Game 3. They lost 108–94 to the Raptors in Toronto, making it 2–1 in the series. Dwight still gave a strong performance, with 19 points and 12 rebounds, but as he said in an interview, "they came out firing on all cylinders and we didn't do a great job of coming back at them."

The Raptors came out swinging the next match, too. The score was knotted near the end of the fourth quarter. Then Nelson, Turkoglu, and Lewis mounted an offensive attack that left the Raptors gasping—and ultimately, on the losing side of the 106–94 score.

The Magic just needed a single win to advance in the playoffs. They hoped to get it in front of their hometown fans in Orlando on April 28.

From the opening tip through to the final seconds, Dwight Howard was a man on a mission. He made a hook, layups, dunks, and free throws. He blocked shots and shoveled assists. He crashed the boards on offense and defense. By game's end, he had 21 points and 21 rebounds for his third 20-20 in the series. Even better, the Magic had the win in their pocket!

The moment the final buzzer sounded, Dwight broke into a broad grin. "It's just an unbelievable feeling," he said joyfully.

It was the first time since 1996 that the Magic had won a playoff series. Now all they had to do was beat their next opponents, the Detroit Pistons.

They didn't do it their first meeting. The Pistons knew how to control the Magic. They controlled Howard, playing an aggressive game that held him to just 12 points and only 8 rebounds.

"Detroit is going to talk and push," Dwight said after the 91–72 loss. "We knew that coming in, but we got too frustrated."

Howard answered the Pistons' physical style of play the next outing. He nabbed 18 rebounds, swatted 2 blocks, and tossed in 22 points. But it was all for nothing. The Magic lost again, 100–93.

That defeat made it nine times in a row that the Pistons had denied the Magic in playoff matches. When the series moved to Orlando, Detriot hoped to make it ten. But they were disappointed.

Rashard Lewis was the hero of Game 3; he fired in 33 of the team's 111 points. Dwight did his share, too, adding 20 points and ripping down 12 rebounds.

"It felt really good finally getting a chance to beat those guys," Howard said later.

Game 4 was a ferocious battle. The Pistons wanted to head back to Detroit with a decisive 3–1 advantage in the series. The Magic wanted to tie the series at two games apiece.

For much of the game, it looked as if Orlando would come out on top. They led by six at the end of the first quarter. At halftime, they had widened the margin to 11. And midway through the third quarter, they were a full 15 points ahead.

But the Pistons didn't roll over and play dead. They tightened their grip on defense and completely shut down the Magic for a full seven minutes while cranking up their own offense. When the third quarter ended, the game was tied 70–70.

The score remained close throughout the fourth quarter. That changed in the final three minutes, when Turkoglu went on a scoring rampage. At 3:05 he hit a three-pointer to make it 83–82 in Orlando's favor. The Pistons pushed past with a pair of free throws, but then Hedo stuck another three-pointer to make it 86–84. Again, Detroit answered with a two-pointer.

It was a tie ball game, with just one minute remaining when Turkoglu struck again, this time with a driving layup. If the Magic could shut down the Pistons' offense — and not make any costly mistakes — they would win!

But it was not to be. Right after Turkoglu's layup, Keyon Dooling fouled Piston Richard Hamilton. Hamilton made both free throws to knot the score yet again. Right after those shots, however, Detroit's

Antonio McDyess committed a foul that sent Jameer Nelson to the line!

In the regular season, Nelson had made 125 out of 151 free throws. He stuck the first of two to put the Magic up by a point. But the second missed!

Pistons and Magic players leaped, hands stretching for the rebound. If Orlando came down with it, they could go right back up and put it through the hoop. Or they could send the ball back out and set up a play.

They didn't get a chance to do either, because Detroit beat them to the ball to give the Pistons control with just forty-three seconds left. They ran down the shot clock as much as they could and then gave the ball to their top scorer, Rasheed Wallace. Wallace missed his jumper, but Detroit recovered the ball again! This time, they made good on their chance with a running jumper by Tayshaun Prince.

Detroit 90, Orlando 89, with eight seconds remaining. The Magic inbounded the ball. Seven seconds ticked away. Turkoglu raced in for a driving layup. He missed! Dwight Howard soared above the rim. His fingers touched the ball for the tip-in. But the ball didn't fall through the hoop! Howard scrambled for the rebound but couldn't control it in time.

Final score: Detroit 90, Orlando 89. Series score: Detroit 3, Orlando 1.

The Pistons hammered in the final nail on the Magic's coffin three nights later before a roaring Michigan crowd. Game 5's 91–86 loss was even more painful for Orlando because they had closed a 10-point deficit to 1 late in the fourth. That was as near as they came to going ahead. Six Detroit foul shots later, the Magic's postseason ended, and the Pistons' celebration began.

Dwight Howard, the player with the perpetual grin, was not smiling.

★ CHAPTER SIXTEEN ★

2008–2009

Beyond Expectations

In early September 2008, Dwight Howard stood before a small crowd in his old high school gymnasium. Around his neck was something he'd always longed for: an Olympic gold medal.

Just two weeks before, Team USA had beaten Spain 118–107 to capture the United States' first gold medal in men's basketball since 2000. Dwight had made five out of nine shots in the final round and averaged 10.9 points and 5.8 rebounds per game overall.

"It's just tight to say that I represented my country," he told the audience. "It's great to know that I'm a part of history."

Of course, Dwight hoped to be part of NBA history, too, by leading the Orlando Magic to their first championship title. He set himself a personal goal to rule the boards, both in rebounding and in blocked shots that season.

The team raced through the early games in November. Howard was a force to be reckoned with, conquering the boards and denying the other team shots. By mid-November, he was leading the league in blocks with an average of 4.2 per game. He was posting double-doubles regularly and on November 12, racked up his first career triple-double, with 30 points, 19 rebounds, and 10 blocked shots.

"I wish he would have had one more rebound. It would have looked really even on the stat sheet — 30, 20, and 10," Magic coach Stan Van Gundy joked after the game. "You can't dominate a game much more than that."

Howard and the Magic continued to dominate throughout the rest of 2008. In December, they lost just three games and won twelve to end with a record of 25 wins and only 7 losses. Unbelievably, they lost just three in January, too, to make their record 35 and 10. It was the best showing by the franchise for several years.

Howard himself had reached his goal of leading

the league in rebounds and blocks. He was also ranked sixth in field goal percentage, a fact that earned him more than three million votes in All-Star balloting.

He hoped to be just as popular when he defended his Slam Dunk title during the All-Star weekend. But that night he wound up on the wrong side of an over-the-top dunk.

The contestants were Nate Robinson of the New York Knicks, Rudy Fernandez of the Portland Trail Blazers, and J. R. Smith of the Denver Nuggets. After the first two-dunk round, Fernandez and Smith were eliminated, leaving Robinson and Howard to duel for the title.

That's when Robinson got a leg up on Howard— or two legs, actually. A day before the Slam Dunk contest, Robinson asked Dwight to help him out with his final dunk. Howard agreed, not knowing what the five-foot-nine guard had in mind. Had he known, he might not have said yes!

Nate positioned Dwight in front of and facing the basket and told him just to stand still so he could jump up and over him on his way to the hoop!

Dwight knew he'd been had. "I thought about

101

turning around and blocking it, like 'I'm not going to let you jump over me,'" he confessed later. "But then I was like, 'Just go ahead, man, it's all for fun.'"

Robinson made the shot, and in doing so, he proved that he was just a bit stronger than "Superman." When the voters dialed in, they awarded the Knick guard the trophy.

Howard took it in stride for the most part. Would he have won if he had refused to let Robinson jump over him? Probably. But as he said later, "I'd given him my word."

Dwight didn't take revenge against Nate, but a few weeks later, he did get a chance to show up someone else who was bent on taking him down a notch.

Shaquille O'Neal had made several unfavorable comments about Dwight that Dwight shrugged off, for the most part. But when he got the opportunity to put Shaq in his place, he took it.

The moment came during a game in early March. Howard and O'Neal both went up for a rebound. Howard came down with it. As he did, his shoulder hit Shaq. Shaq went down, and he went down hard!

"Yeah, I flopped," Shaq confessed later. To add insult to injury, Dwight dunked the ball.

By March 25, Orlando had secured the Southeast Division title by beating the 2008 NBA champions, the Boston Celtics. Dwight was virtually unstoppable that night, posting 24 points, 21 rebounds, 4 blocks, 2 assists, and 2 steals. Unbelievably, half of his points and rebounds came in just the first twelve minutes of play! That game was his eighth 20-20 game of the season. Only three other players had had more 20-20 games in a single season.

And Howard wasn't through yet. On March 30, he surpassed Wilt Chamberlain to become the youngest player to post 5,000 career rebounds. Five nights later, he added a ninth 20-20 game with 21 points and 23 rebounds. He also had a game-high 5 assists, plus 4 blocks and 3 steals.

The Magic's season ended with a win over the Charlotte Bobcats. That victory brought their record to 59 and 23, the second best ever in the history of the franchise and good enough for the third seed in the Eastern Conference playoffs.

"If we play consistent basketball," Dwight Howard predicted of their chances in the postseason, "we can beat anybody."

✶ CHAPTER SEVENTEEN ✶
Playoffs 2009

Into the Finals

Rashard Lewis had tendinitis in his right knee. Hedo Turkoglu had a sprained left ankle. Jameer Nelson had missed the second half of the season with a severe shoulder injury. With three of the five starters out of the lineup, many wondered if the Magic stood a chance in the playoffs.

They needn't have worried. While Nelson was unable to play, both Lewis and Turkoglu were back in action when the first round began on April 19. First up were the Philadelphia 76ers. The Magic had bested the Sixers in all three meetings that year. They hoped to sweep them in this series.

They didn't. In Game 1, Philadelphia had the edge throughout most of the first half. Orlando took control in the third quarter, going up by as many as 17 points. Many of those points came from Dwight

Howard, who recorded a career playoff high of 31, plus 16 rebounds, 2 assists, and 2 blocks—despite being sidelined for several minutes after being scratched across his eyes by a defender.

But the Sixers rallied early in the fourth. The Magic seemed powerless to stop the onslaught; at the thirty-four-second mark, the score was tied at 98 each.

It stayed that way for the next twenty-two seconds. Then, with just two seconds showing on the clock, Sixer Andre Iguodala sank one from eighteen feet out. Turkoglu tried to get the Magic up and over with a buzzer-beating three-pointer, but the shot missed. Final score: Philadelphia 100, Orlando 98.

To lose after being ahead by such a great margin was a crushing blow to Dwight Howard. Fortunately, he got a big morale boost two nights later, when the NBA announced that he had been voted the Defensive Player of the Year. He was the youngest player in league history to win the award, and only the fifth player to win it for both his rebounding (13.8 per game) and his blocked shots (2.9 per game).

He was all smiles when he accepted the bronze trophy. He noted afterward that he had set a goal before the season to become a better defensive player so that he could help his teammates out. He also added that he believed they had a chance to win the championship.

The Magic got closer to that chance when they beat the Sixers 96–87 the next night—although they nearly gave up the game again when they let an 18-point lead slip through their fingers.

"Man, I hope these boys don't come back again," Howard commented afterward.

Philadelphia did come back, however, despite a monstrous performance by Dwight, who earned a new career playoff high of 36 points plus 11 rebounds. It was all for nothing: The Sixers snatched Game 3 away from Orlando in the final seconds with a score of 96–94.

It was a tie game in the last moments of the next meeting, too. But this time the Magic got the upper hand thanks to an outstanding shot from Turkoglu at the one-second mark. Final score: Orlando 84, Philadelphia 81.

The teams were now even at two games apiece.

Dwight Howard made sure the Magic went ahead in the series by delivering a personal best performance of 24 playoff rebounds, as well as 24 points, in the 91–78 Game 5 victory.

He also delivered something else that game: a sharp elbow to Sixer Samuel Dalembert's head. While play often gets physical in the paint, purposefully injuring an opponent is grounds for suspension.

Howard defended himself by saying he had no intention of hurting anyone but was simply playing aggressively. And in fact, he injured one of his own teammates, Courtney Lee, later in the game when his elbow hit Lee's head during a block.

Unfortunately, when officials reviewed the replays of Howard's elbow swing, they decided that Howard had struck him on purpose. He was suspended from playing in Game 6; the Magic would have to play without their star, as well as Lee, who needed surgery.

As it turned out, that game was the highest scoring for Orlando yet. They won easily, 114–89, to advance to the second round. There, they would meet the defending NBA champions, the Boston Celtics.

⋆ CHAPTER EIGHTEEN ⋆

Playoffs 2009

Celtics and Cavs

Dwight Howard couldn't wait to get back into the lineup for the first match against the Celtics. That game was similar to Game 1 of the Magic-Sixers series in that Orlando nearly blew a huge lead to lose. They were up by 28 points early in the third quarter and were still ahead by 16 when the fourth quarter began.

Then they fell apart. In five and a half minutes, they scored just 6 points while giving up 11. A pair of Celtics three-pointers with three minutes remaining narrowed the score to Orlando 89, Boston 83; another in the final seconds tightened it even more, to 93–90. But that three-pointer was the Celtics' last basket of the game. Final score: Orlando 95, Boston 90.

There was no such collapse the next game, but only because the Magic failed to capture the lead even once. With their 112–94 victory, the Celtics tied the series at one apiece.

Dwight Howard went into Game 3 determined to get a win. He succeeded, delivering 17 points and 14 rebounds in the 117–96 victory. But it was as a shot blocker that he made the most impact. He walloped away four in the first quarter alone to force the Celtics into taking jump shots instead of layups or dunks. On his fifth swat, he jumped so high he had to brace himself with his left hand on the backboard before sending the ball careening into the stands.

"It starts with me," the Defensive Player of the Year stated. "I have to do that every night if we want to be successful."

Game 4 started off as a complete hack-fest for both sides. Twenty-nine fouls were called in the first half alone. The lead seesawed throughout, with neither team gaining a huge advantage. The match was decided with less than a second left on the clock — and by an unexpected player.

Celtic Glen Davis had come off the bench for an injured Kevin Garnett midway through the regular season. He'd played well in the series so far but hadn't been a major player. That changed when he shot a twenty-one-foot jumper buzzer-beater to give Boston the 95–94 win.

Boston won the next game, too, once again coming back from a big deficit to leave the Magic in the dust. That made it twice in the series and five times in the postseason that Orlando had allowed a double-digit lead to slip through their fingers. Four of those games had ended in defeat. Something had to change for the Magic before it happened again.

Something did, although the way the change came about didn't make everybody happy. After the Game 5 loss, a frustrated Dwight Howard criticized Stan Van Gundy's coaching strategy, saying that the offense should be focused on getting the ball to him. He later apologized.

To his teammates and Orlando fans, he had a different message: "We can't give up hope. We're in this series to win it. We're going to win this series."

Those were bold statements, but they turned out to be true. Dwight dominated in Game 6, posting his fifth career postseason 20-20 game with 23 points and 22 rebounds in the Magic's 83–75 win. He wasn't as commanding in Game 7, yet he still added 12 points and 16 rebounds. He also showed everyone why he had won the Defensive Player of the Year award by swatting away five of Boston's shots. Had he not done so, the final score of Magic 101, Celtics 82 might have looked a whole lot different.

"Wow, we just knocked off the defending champs on their home court," Dwight wrote in his blog a few days later. "How about that?????"

With the Celtics put behind them, the Magic turned their attention to their next opponents. The Cleveland Cavaliers had been a powerhouse team ever since LeBron James joined their roster. James had scored no fewer than 25 points in the postseason so far and had recently tallied almost half of his team's points in a win over the Atlanta Hawks. Behind his might, the Cavs had swept both squads they had faced in the playoffs. Now they looked to use the same broom on Orlando.

Cleveland fans couldn't wait to watch their home team show Orlando the door. And in Game 1, it looked like they'd get what they came for. The Cavs took and held an early lead in the first quarter. All five of Cleveland's starters added to the score, proving how well they worked together as a team.

On the Magic's side, Dwight led the charge with

five out of seven shots finding their mark for 10 points. The first of those was a dunk that was so powerful that it caused the shot clock on top of the backboard to fall over!

"I guess I don't know my own strength sometimes," Dwight chuckled after the game.

Unfortunately, not every Magic player was shooting as well. At the end of the first quarter, the score was Cleveland 33, Orlando 19.

In the second quarter, LeBron James got white-hot. He stuck shots from inside, outside, and the free-throw line. His teammates followed suit to give them another 30 points for their side. Orlando chalked up nearly as many, but that was nowhere near enough to overcome the first quarter deficit.

Stan Van Gundy tore into his players in the locker room during halftime. "You're all witnesses!" Dwight recalled him saying about the way they were standing around while LeBron scored at will.

That simple statement put a fire in the Magic players' bellies. They roared through the third quarter to come within four points. Then, in the opening minute of the fourth, they made seven unanswered points to take the lead!

But the game wasn't over yet. The Cavs drew even. Then, at 5:07, Turkoglu stuck a three-pointer to put them ahead 93–90. LeBron drove in and dunked to tighten it to 93–92. The two players exchanged driving layups in the next two possessions to make it 95–94. Then Rashard Lewis hit a three-point jumper. So did Cav Mo Williams. For every shot the Magic took, the Cavs had an answer until, with forty seconds on the clock, Cleveland drilled in a go-ahead three-pointer! Cavs 103, Magic 102.

Orlando called a full timeout. When play resumed, Magic guard Rafer Alston got the ball to Lewis. Lewis shot from sixteen feet out and scored! But unbelievably, LeBron James scored, too, and he was fouled—by Dwight Howard! It was Howard's sixth for the game, sending him to the bench to watch the conclusion from the sidelines. It was also a costly error that resulted in another point for the Cavs to give them a 106–104 lead.

There were still twenty-five seconds left in the game, however. That's plenty of time for a team to set up a play and get off a final shot. That's just what the Magic did. Turkoglu rifled the ball over to Lewis, who launched a three-pointer that kissed the glass and swished the net strings! Fourteen seconds later, the game ended with the final score of Magic 107, Cavs 106.

"Now will people believe we are here to play and here to win this thing?" Dwight asked.

Sadly, Orlando didn't "win this thing" when the two teams next met. Instead, they found themselves on the wrong side of an amazing, buzzer-beating, game-winning three-pointer from the fingertips of LeBron James. "I've seen him do some crazy things," Dwight blogged admiringly after the 96–95 loss, "but that was the sickest of them all!"

The Magic were down, but not beaten—not by a long shot. They hustled their way to a decisive 99–89 win in Game 3. Howard had 24 points for the night, 14 of which were free throws, a testament to how hard he'd been working on that particular shot.

Game 4 was an overtime nail-biter. The two teams were evenly matched throughout regulation play, but in the extra minutes, Dwight Howard took control. He slammed home back-to-back dunks, lofted in a layup, tipped the ball in for two more points, and sank two free throws for 10 of Orlando's total 16 points. The Cavs dropped behind but then caught up in the last minute.

Almost caught up, that is. Final score: Orlando 116, Cleveland 114. The Magic needed just one more win to advance to the NBA Finals.

They didn't get it the next game. LeBron James and the Cavs chewed them up and spit them out to take Game 5, 112–102. But the match after that, it was all Magic, all night long — and Dwight Howard led the way.

Five dunks, twelve out of sixteen free throws, plus layups, hook shots, jumpers, and bank shots. Howard was hitting from all over the floor until by night's end, he had tallied 40 points, the most of his postseason career. He didn't spend all his time shooting, though. He also crashed the boards for 14 rebounds, assisted on four other baskets, and walloped away one of Cleveland's attempted shots.

At game's end, the scoreboard said it all: Orlando Magic 103, Cleveland Cavaliers 90.

"We're going to the NBA Finals!!!" Even in his blog, Dwight's excitement and joy shone through. "Let me say it again so it can really soak in deep: **WE'RE GOING TO THE NBA FINALS!!!**"

★ CHAPTER NINETEEN ★

Finals 2009

Finally in the Finals

The Magic's playoff run hadn't been easy. The Philadelphia 76ers had been tough. The Boston Celtics had been tougher. The Cleveland Cavaliers had been the toughest of all—until the Orlando Magic faced the Los Angeles Lakers, that is.

This was the Lakers' thirtieth trip to the NBA Finals, more times than any other team in the league. They'd won fourteen titles, the last in 2002. They had come close to winning again in 2008, but were defeated by the Boston Celtics. Now they returned with many of the same superstar players, including the NBA's newest Most Valuable Player, Kobe Bryant. All were hungry to add a fifteenth banner to their arena rafters.

By comparison, the Magic had only been to the Finals one time before. That was in 1995, when they lost 4–0 to the Houston Rockets. Obviously, their roster had changed completely since then. Yet their current lineup was filled with top talent, and if the teams' two regular season meetings were any indication, there was a very real possibility that Orlando could beat out Los Angeles for the ring.

The Magic had won both of those matches, although the margin by which they had won was small. Still, it proved that they could power past the mighty Lakers. They were confident they could do it again in the Finals.

Their confidence took a severe beating in Game 1, unfortunately.

The match was played at the Staples Center in Los Angeles before a crowd of more than eighteen thousand cheering Lakers fans. Those fans expected to witness a blowout by their team. After the first quarter, however, their cheers turned a bit quieter, for the score was nearly even at Magic 24, Lakers 22. They were subdued through the early minutes of the second quarter, too, when Orlando kept the lead.

That changed four minutes into the second

quarter. The Lakers returned from a full time-out and took over the game. Luke Walton made back-to-back jumpers. Kobe Bryant stuck three long bombs in a row to make it ten unanswered points — and the Lakers weren't done yet.

By halftime, the Lakers were up by ten points. In a punishing third quarter, they held the Magic to just 15 points while adding 29 to their side of the board. Neither team cracked 20 points in the final twelve minutes of play, but by then the Lakers had run away with the game. Final score: Los Angeles 100, Orlando 75.

How had the Lakers done it? One strategy was to control Dwight Howard by covering him with two and sometimes three men. They executed that strategy so well that he took only six shots that night. Of those six, only one made it through the hoop. The rest of his 12 points came from free throws.

Howard was effective on defense, pulling down 15 rebounds and blocking 2 shots. Without his efforts there, the score might have looked a whole lot worse for the Magic.

Los Angeles now had the upper hand. But the Magic weren't beaten yet. After falling behind in the first half of Game 2, they charged forward to take a two-point lead late in the game. Rashard Lewis led that charge by scoring two free throws, assisting Hedo Turkoglu with his 23-foot jumper, and assisting Dwight Howard with his slam dunk. Rafer Alston, Mickael Pietrus, and Jameer Nelson also helped bring the Magic's score up 30 points in the third quarter.

The teams battled for the advantage throughout much of the fourth quarter. Neither succeeded in capturing it, although the Magic came very close in a play that was featured on the sports highlights over and over again.

The score was knotted at 88 apiece when Orlando called a time-out. After a quick discussion on the sidelines, Turkoglu took the ball out of bounds at half court. The referee blew his whistle. Courtney Lee raced to the hoop. Turkoglu lobbed a pass to him. Lee caught the ball cleanly but was running so fast that he overshot his layup. The ball ricocheted off the glass and bounced to the floor. The game would be decided in overtime.

Dwight started the ball rolling for the Magic with a three-point play two minutes into the extra period.

The Lakers answered with seven points of their own to go up 97–91. As time ticked down, Lewis got the ball and dished it to J. J. Redick under the hoop. Redick laid the ball in for two points to make it 97–93. But once again, Los Angeles upped their side of the score—and this time, it was Dwight's fault. He fouled Laker Pau Gasol when the ball squirted loose. Gasol went to the line and made both free throws.

But all was not lost. With just twenty-six seconds on the clock, Lewis snared the ball and hit a basket from outside the arc! With the score at Lakers 99, Magic 96 and time still left to go, a second overtime period looked possible.

It didn't happen. Laker Lamar Odom was fouled and made both his foul shots. The final score was Los Angeles 101, Orlando 96.

Dwight had had a good game overall, with 17 points, 16 rebounds, 4 assists, 4 steals, and 4 blocks. He was the second player in NBA history since Hakeem Olajuwon in 1986 to earn such high marks in these five stat categories. But he also committed seven of the team's twenty turnovers.

"I've just got to do a better job of finding my

teammates and being aware of the guards coming in the paint for strips," he wrote in his blog. "Tough, tough loss...[but] it's not over yet."

The series moved to Orlando for Game 3. Back on their home court, the Magic were not to be denied. They found their shooting touch early on, hitting 75 percent of their shots in the first half for an NBA Finals record.

But somehow, the Lakers emerged on top, 31–27, after the first twelve minutes. After that, the score ping-ponged back and forth throughout the remaining thirty-six minutes. Many fans began to wonder if yet another overtime decision was looming.

They got their answer in the last thirty seconds of the match. That's when Howard stole the ball from Bryant. Mickael Pietrus was fouled and made both of his shots to put the Magic ahead 106–102. The Lakers tried to tighten the gap but missed four out of four three-pointers before Bryant caught his own rebound and snuck in a layup. Then Bryant fouled Lewis, sending him to the line. He made both count. Final score: Magic 108, Lakers 104.

Howard had fulfilled his vow to control his turn-overs that night. He ended with just one. His other stats were just as strong: 21 points, 14 rebounds, 2 assists, 2 blocks, and 1 steal. He was delighted to have helped his team to the win, but was even happier that the team had played so well together. "We were patient, we were confident, and we played with a swagger again," he blogged. "We ain't no pushovers."

The Magic certainly weren't "pushovers" the next game, either. Powered by incredible rebounding and blocking by Dwight, plus on-target shooting from the starting lineup, they motored ahead of the Lakers by 12 points by halftime. Howard punctuated his determination to win with an immense slam dunk at the start of the third quarter.

Those were his only points of that period, unfortunately. The Lakers shut down the Magic's offense, holding them to just 14 points in the third quarter, while scoring more than twice that number themselves to go up by four at the end of the twelve minutes!

The Magic fought back against the Lakers' scoring tidal wave to tie it all up, 75–75, at the five-minute mark in the fourth quarter. Pietrus gave them a one-point edge with a free throw, but the Lakers swooped in and scored twice to go up by four. Then, with four and a half minutes remaining in the game— *boom!*—Dwight thundered down a rim-rattling dunk. And when Turkoglu stuck a free throw and Dwight chalked in a two-pointer followed by a foul shot, the Magic were once more in the lead!

Unbelievably, Los Angeles closed the gap in the final thirty seconds of the game. That gap might have been wider had Dwight made even one of two free throws at the eleven-second mark. But he missed both, and when the time ran out, the score was tied.

Game 4, like Game 2, was decided in overtime. The Magic rallied as best they could, but the Lakers made the shots when they counted the most. The final score of the game was 99–91.

"I don't know what to say," Dwight apologized to his fans online later. "I have been working so hard on my free throws, and making a lot of progress the last couple of weeks, but last night just wasn't my night."

His poor free throwing aside, Dwight had had a monstrous game: 16 points, 21 boards, and 9 blocked shots, the most of any NBA Finals game.

That it had all been for nothing made him miserable, but not defeated. "Nobody is hurting more about what happened last night than me," he said. "But I'll tell you this: we ain't quitting now."

The Magic didn't quit—but they didn't win the next game, either. After a very strong first quarter in which they leaped ahead by 9 points, they were flattened by the Lakers, who went on a 16–0 scoring spree midway through the second quarter. Los Angeles maintained a double-digit lead for much of the remainder of the game. In the end, Orlando simply couldn't stop them.

Final score: Los Angeles Lakers 99, Orlando Magic 86.

While the Lakers celebrated their fifteenth championship title, Dwight and Jameer Nelson sat on the sidelines, watching. "It hurts," Dwight said, not a trace of a smile on his face. "It hurts a lot."

But it was pain with a purpose: They wanted to carry the image of the Lakers' celebration with them into the off-season as a way of motivating them to work harder.

Later, in front of the cameras during the postgame press conference, Dwight complimented his teammates for getting to the Finals, adding that few people outside of the team had believed they could go so far that season. He was also gracious in his praise of the Lakers, particularly Kobe Bryant, and admitted that Los Angeles had been the better team overall.

In response to a question about whether he thought they could return to the Finals in 2010, Dwight's natural optimism shone through loud and clear: "I've got a great feeling that we'll have a chance to be back," he said with a hint of a smile. "There's no doubt in my mind about that."

✶ CHAPTER TWENTY ✶
2009 and Beyond

A Blessing

Dwight Howard has been working hard at his game ever since losing to the Lakers in 2009. But he hasn't spent every minute on the court. His growing celebrity, his generous nature, and his outstanding athleticism have led him down paths he'd only dreamed of walking.

His charitable activities began in his rookie season, when he founded the Dwight D. Howard Foundation with his parents. The goal of the Foundation is to provide low-income students with scholarships to Southwest Atlanta Christian Academy and financial assistance to middle schools in Orlando.

Since then, Dwight has been involved in many local and international relief efforts. In 2005, he was named the recipient of the Rich and Helen DeVos

Community Enrichment Award, an award given annually to the Magic player who dedicates time to improving the lives of people in the Orlando community. Dwight had spent many hours that year visiting local schools and talking with children during Read to Achieve events.

"It was fun!" Dwight said enthusiastically. "I am definitely going to keep it up."

In more recent years, he hosted a summer basketball camp with the Boys and Girls Clubs of Central Florida and the YMCA and took children on shopping sprees at toy stores. He helped build a playground. He visited sick children in hospitals and donated money to buy backpacks stuffed with school supplies.

In September 2009, he joined other NBA players for the Basketball Without Borders (BWB) program in South Africa. There, he took part in several basketball events geared at raising awareness of that country's health, education, and wellness issues. He worked to help off the court, too, by laying cement for a house being built and planting a garden.

Dwight has been busy with other activities, too. He has appeared in several very funny commercials, in two movies, on a late-night talk show, as a guest star on a home improvement show, and on many magazine covers. He's also the star of a basketball video game, *NBA Live 10*, a fact that delights him.

"I was going crazy!" he said after he found out he'd been chosen as the cover image. "I've wanted to be on the cover of *NBA Live* since I was a kid."

When he's not posing for photos, being filmed, or appearing as a cartoon version of himself in a video game, he's keeping in touch with his huge fan base through online social networks. He spends much of his free time relaxing in his home in Orlando, a huge house filled with the latest video and gaming equipment, more bedrooms than he knows what to do with, and even a closet dedicated to his favorite candy, Skittles, M&M'S, and Starburst.

Dwight's dedication to God and the church has remained strong throughout his five-year career in the NBA. When in Atlanta, he attends services at the Fellowship of Faith Church. He also prays regularly before games.

But even one as committed to his religion as Dwight is can falter at times. In 2008, he became a father to a little boy named Braylon, although he was not married to Braylon's mother. He suffered some backlash from this, and yet, he was very open about how he felt about the new person in his life.

"A blessing," he calls Braylon, echoing his own father's description of himself so many years ago. "When I first saw him, I had to turn away from him for a second. Just looking at him and looking in his eyes and seeing the innocence of a little baby...I cried."

A blessing is what many Orlando fans call Dwight himself. In the six years he has been on the team, he has raised the Magic to greater heights than any other player in decades. While a 2010 bid for the championship title ended in disappointment for the Magic, Howard continues to give Orlando hope for a future Finals victory. His energy and power lead him to routinely turn in performances of 30 or more points and double-digit rebounding stats. His drive to win has raised the team to greater heights than any other player has in decades.

And through it all, Howard brings his own brand of fun to the court. He can't help it. "Basketball gives me joy," he once said to his father. "Why shouldn't I be having fun?"

Dwight Howard's Year-to-Year Statistics

Regular Season

Year	Team	GP	GS	MPG	FG%	3P%	FT%	RPG	APG	SPG	BPG	PPG
2004–05	Orlando	82	82	32.6	0.520	0.000	0.671	10.0	0.9	0.9	1.7	12.0
2005–06	Orlando	82	81	36.8	0.531	0.000	0.595	12.5	1.5	0.8	1.4	15.8
2006–07	Orlando	82	82	36.9	0.603	0.500	0.586	12.3	1.9	0.9	1.9	17.6
2007–08	Orlando	82	82	37.7	0.599	0.000	0.590	14.2	1.3	0.9	2.2	20.7
2008–09	Orlando	79	79	35.7	0.572	0.000	0.594	13.8	1.4	1.0	2.9	20.6
Career		407	406	35.9	0.565	0.091	0.607	12.5	1.4	0.9	2.0	17.3
All-Star		3	2	26.3	0.688	0.000	0.385	10.0	1.3	1.3	1.7	16.3

Playoffs

Year	Team	GP	GS	MPG	FG%	3P%	FT%	RPG	APG	SPG	BPG	PPG
2006–07	Orlando	4	4	41.8	0.548	0.000	0.455	14.8	1.8	0.5	1.0	15.2
2007–08	Orlando	10	10	42.1	0.581	0.000	0.542	15.8	0.9	0.8	3.4	18.9
2008–09	Orlando	23	23	39.3	0.601	0.000	0.636	15.3	1.9	0.9	2.6	20.3
Career		37	37	40.3	0.590	0.000	0.596	15.4	1.6	0.8	2.6	19.4

Dwight Howard's Year-to-Year Highlights

2003–2004

- Member of the Southwest Atlanta Christian Academy Georgia state championship team
- 2004 Naismith Prep Player of the Year
- 2004 Morgan Wooten High School Player of the Year
- 2004 Gatorade National Player of the Year
- Georgia's Mr. Basketball 2004
- 2004 McDonald's National High School Player of the Year
- Co-MVP of the 2004 McDonald's All-American High School Game (with teammate Josh Smith)
- Member of the *PARADE* magazine All-America Team
- Number one NBA draft pick

2004–2005

- Youngest player in NBA history to record a double-double average (12 points per game, 10 rebounds per game)
- Youngest player in NBA history to record double digits in rebounds for a season
- Youngest player in NBA history to record a 20-rebound game
- First prep-to-pro player in NBA history to start in all 82 regular season games
- Member of the NBA's All-Rookie First Team
- Participated in the got milk? Rookie Challenge

2005–2006

- Youngest player in NBA history to lead the league in rebounds
- Tied for second place for most double-doubles (60) in a single season

2006–2007

- Member of the East All-Star Team
- Helped Orlando Magic to first playoff appearance since 2003

2007–2008
- Winner of the Slam Dunk contest
- Helped Orlando Magic to first division title since 1996

August 2008
- Member of the gold medal–winning Team USA in the 2008 Summer Olympics in Beijing, China

2008–2009
- Member of the East All-Star Team
- 2009 Defensive Player of the Year, the youngest player in NBA history to be so honored
- Helped Orlando Magic reach the NBA Finals for the first time since 1995

Milestones and Records

- Youngest player in NBA history to reach:
  - 3,000 rebounds
  - 4,000 rebounds
  - 5,000 rebounds
- Youngest player in NBA history to record double digits in rebounds for a season
- Youngest player in NBA history to record a 20-rebound game
- Highest career field goal percentage in All-Star Game history: 0.810 (17 field goals made of 21 attempts)
- Youngest player in NBA history to lead the league in rebounding at 22 years, 130 days (14.2 rebounds per game throughout 2007–2008 season)

- Youngest player in NBA history to lead the league in blocks at 23 years, 128 days (2.9 blocks per game throughout 2008–2009 season)
- NBA Finals record (in a game) of 9 blocks, vs. Los Angeles Lakers, June 11, 2009

THE #1
SPORTS SERIES
FOR KIDS

Read them all!

*Previously published as Crackerjack Halfback

Lacrosse Face-Off

Lacrosse Firestorm

Line Drive to Short**

Long-Arm Quarterback

Long Shot for Paul

Look Who's Playing First Base

Miracle at the Plate

Mountain Bike Mania

Nothin' But Net

Out at Second

Penalty Shot

Power Pitcher***

The Reluctant Pitcher

Return of the Home Run Kid

Run for It

Shoot for the Hoop

Shortstop from Tokyo

Skateboard Renegade

Skateboard Tough

Slam Dunk

Snowboard Champ

Snowboard Maverick

Snowboard Showdown

Soccer Duel

Soccer Halfback

Soccer Hero

Soccer Scoop

Stealing Home

The Submarine Pitch

The Team That Couldn't Lose

Tennis Ace

Tight End

Top Wing

Touchdown for Tommy

Tough to Tackle

Wingman on Ice

The Year Mom Won the Pennant

All available in paperback from Little, Brown and Company
**Previously published as Pressure Play
***Previously published as Baseball Pals

Matt Christopher®

Sports Bio Bookshelf

Muhammad Ali	Randy Johnson
Lance Armstrong	Michael Jordan
Kobe Bryant	Peyton and Eli Manning
Jennifer Capriati	Yao Ming
Dale Earnhardt Sr.	Shaquille O'Neal
Jeff Gordon	Albert Pujols
Ken Griffey Jr.	Jackie Robinson
Mia Hamm	Alex Rodriguez
Tony Hawk	Babe Ruth
Dwight Howard	Curt Schilling
Ichiro	Sammy Sosa
LeBron James	Tiger Woods
Derek Jeter	